THE MAKING OF
A NAVY SEAL

THE MAKING OF A NAVY SEAL

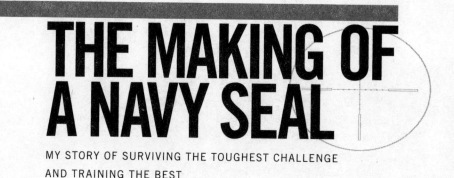

MY STORY OF SURVIVING THE TOUGHEST CHALLENGE AND TRAINING THE BEST

BRANDON WEBB

AND

JOHN DAVID MANN

FOREWORD BY MARCUS LUTTRELL

ST. MARTIN'S PRESS ✹ NEW YORK

THE MAKING OF A NAVY SEAL. Copyright © 2015 by Brandon Webb and John David Mann. Foreword copyright © 2015 by Marcus Luttrell. All rights reserved. Printed in the United States of America. For information, address St. Martin's Press, 175 Fifth Avenue, New York, N.Y. 10010.

www.stmartins.com

Designed by Omar Chapa
Maps by Emily Langmade

Library of Congress Cataloging-in-Publication Data

Webb, Brandon.
    The making of a Navy SEAL : my story of surviving the toughest challenge and training the best / Brandon Webb with John David Mann; foreword by Marcus Luttrell. — First edition.
        p. cm.
    ISBN 978-1-250-06942-9 (hardcover)
    ISBN 978-1-250-08708-9 (Scholastic Edition)
    ISBN 978-1-4668-7833-4 (e-book)
    1. Webb, Brandon.   2. United States. Navy. SEALs—Biography.
3. United States. Navy. SEALs—Physical training.   4. United States. Navy—Commando troops—Training of.   5. Afghan War, 2001—Personal narratives, American.   6. War on Terrorism, 2001–2009—Personal narratives, American.   7. California, Southern—Biography.   I. Mann, John David.   II. Title.
    VG87.W429 2015
    359.9'84—dc23
    [B]

                                                                        2015016246

St. Martin's Griffin books may be purchased for educational, business, or promotional use. For information on bulk purchases, please contact the Macmillan Corporate and Premium Sales Department at 1-800-221-7945, extension 5442, or write to specialmarkets@macmillan.com.

First Edition: August 2015

10   9   8   7   6   5   4   3   2   1

For my three children

CONTENTS

Foreword ix

Modern Warfare xiii

A Word from the Author xvii

Part One: Born Ready for Action 1

Part Two: Boot Camp Training 29

Part Three: Becoming a Navy SEAL 55

Part Four: One of America's Deadliest Snipers 97

Part Five: Duty Calls 135

Part Six: Continuing to Protect and Defend 175

Epilogue 209

Glossary 215

Acknowledgments 219

Index 223

FOREWORD

I first met Brandon Webb when I was a student in the Naval Special Warfare sniper course. Sniper school was one of the toughest things I've ever done. In some ways it was even more difficult than the Basic Underwater Demolition/SEAL training (BUD/S), that every SEAL undergoes. The sniper course starts with a stalking phase, which is all about stealth and concealment. We are trained to crawl painstaking inches and yards undetected across enemy-held territory. I have to be honest: this was not easy for me. The shooting part came naturally. The stalking part did not. I'm a pretty big guy, and trying to make myself look like a plant or bush instead of a six-foot-tall Texan . . . it just wasn't happening. I don't know how I would have gotten through it if it weren't for Brandon being my instructor. Brandon and his team were incredibly tough on us. They were intent on making us some of the best special operations forces in the field. And they succeeded. It wasn't just a matter of making our lives hard. Brandon went beyond the call. He set aside time after course hours to answer questions and work with all the students. He mentored me, and did whatever it took to make sure I knew my stuff.

Graduating sniper school was one of the proudest achievements of my life.

I went from sniper school almost directly to Afghanistan. Not too many months after being in Brandon's class, on June 29, 2005, I found myself in the soaring Hindu Kush mountains, a subrange of the Himalayas, not far from the Afghanistan-Pakistan border. Everyone else in my recon team was gone, including my brother Morgan's best friend, Matt "Axe" Axelson—all killed by the same couple hundred Taliban forces who were now doing their level best to kill me, too. If it had not been for Brandon's patience, care, and skill with me in the sniper course not long before, I can promise you this: I would have left these Texan bones bleaching on that hillside.

Brandon's training saved my life then, just as it would again several years later in a very different environment, fighting house to house on the hot, muggy streets of Iraq.

And I know I'm not the only one. There are a lot of people out there, people whose names you'll never hear, who are alive today because of the efforts, skill, and dedication of Brandon and others like him. What you're about to read is not just the story of the making of a Navy SEAL sniper but the story of one guy who went on to help shape the lives of hundreds of elite special operations warriors.

It was a great honor to serve on and off the battlefield with the men of the U.S. Navy SEAL teams and U.S. SOCOM (Special Operations Command). Brandon and I have both lost many good friends over the years, and it's comforting to know that the memories of these great warriors will live on in the stories we share with you. My hope is that you will come to know them as intimately as we did, and that you will continue to pass on their stories of heroism so that we may never forget the ultimate sacrifice they made for the freedoms we enjoy today.

Brandon has a great story to tell, and it is living proof that you

can achieve anything you put your mind to. It's an honor to intro-
duce his memoir.

Never quit.

Marcus Luttrell (USN Ret.), Navy SEAL and bestselling author
of *Lone Survivor*

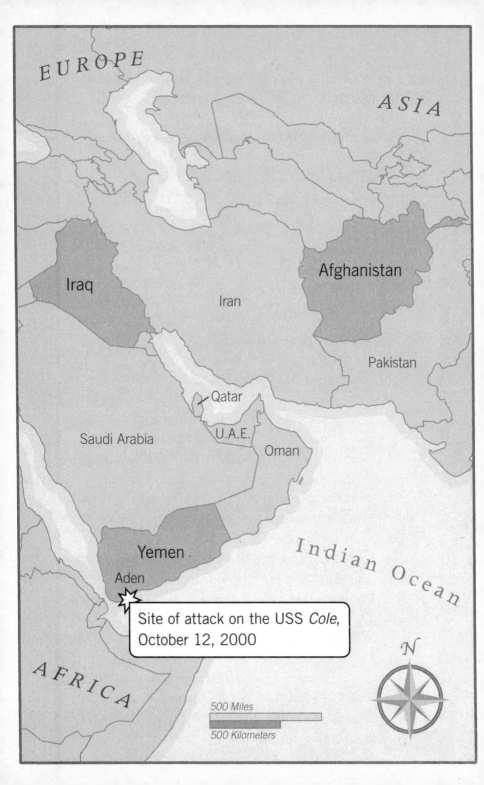

EUROPE

ASIA

Iraq

Iran

Afghanistan

Pakistan

Qatar

Saudi Arabia

U.A.E.

Oman

Yemen

Aden

Site of attack on the USS *Cole*,
October 12, 2000

Indian Ocean

AFRICA

N

500 Miles

500 Kilometers

MODERN WARFARE

Beginning with ancient times and continuing throughout the twentieth century, war had always been a matter of hurling masses of men and military equipment against one another. The bigger the tank, the aircraft, or the naval destroyer, and the more men you deployed, the greater your chances of victory were.

Then came October 12, 2000. On this date, the USS *Cole*, a naval destroyer, was refueling in Aden, Yemen. Two suicide bombers piloting a small speedboat full of explosives attacked the ship. Seventeen crew members died, another thirty-nine were injured, and the huge ship was severely crippled. The attack on the USS *Cole* opened my eyes to how ill prepared we were for the threat that existed everywhere around us. This was not just a catastrophe, and it wasn't just about whether we were adequately prepared for surprise attacks. There was a fundamental shift happening here, a shift in the very nature of military conflict, and this attack off the coast of Yemen was arguably its wake-up call.

There was a crew of nearly three hundred on board the *Cole*. There was no comparison between it and the small speedboat with just two individuals on board. As weapons of war go, it doesn't get much more massive than a billion-dollar destroyer—but it had just been nearly sunk by two guys in a dinky little speedboat. Clearly the number of men and the size of military equipment were no longer all that mattered.

There was no turning back and no ignoring it any longer. We had definitely entered the age of asymmetrical warfare. That is, with the attack on the USS *Cole*, we had fully and violently entered the age of a new kind of war, one in which the weaker opponent in a conflict uses terrorism in an attempt to gain an advantage.

The years following the attack on the *Cole* saw a radical shift take place in the makeup of the U.S. Department of Defense, especially in relation to its special operations forces. In the long story of war, special operations—the British and Australian Special Air Service; the American Green Berets, Army Rangers, and Navy SEALs—were exactly that: special, something you didn't use every day. Spec ops forces were kept on the shelf and brought out for deployment only in certain circumstances. Those of us in spec ops were the icing on the cake of massive destruction, the period at the end of a sentence of overwhelming forces. Special operations were there mainly to support the larger mission.

Now that equation has changed. Today, the relationship has been turned virtually on its head. Over the first part of the twenty-first century, the entire strategy of American military organization has shifted toward one in which our massive assets, such as destroyers, aircraft carriers, and nuclear submarines, have been reconfigured to support small spec ops field teams and units. The spec ops warrior of the twentieth century was fundamentally an outsider who worked on the edges of military strategy. Today he stands at its core.

As for the terrorists, who are they? Al Qaeda, a militant Islamic extremist organization founded by Osama bin Laden, was

A WORD FROM THE AUTHOR

What I wouldn't give to be twelve years old again, but, this time, with the knowledge that I have now as a Navy SEAL. (Plus, the video games are a lot cooler today than they were more than thirty years ago when I was playing Mario on my Nintendo.) I can't go back in time, but I can give *you* some tips that I wish I'd had when I was about your age.

Life isn't easy. This is something I know most of you already understand by now. There are always challenges. Parents get divorced, you change schools, and there's bullying, annoying brothers and sisters, making new friends, and not getting picked first for the team to name just a few of them. The good news is that if you start thinking differently about all these challenges you can use them to help fuel an inner fire that will drive you to pursue your ultimate dreams in life. Really.

When I was young my parents got divorced, I changed schools a lot, got behind on my grades, my sister annoyed me, and, to make things worse, I lived on a

sailboat! Kids laughed and made fun of me on my floating "trailer."
I could have felt sorry for myself, but I learned early on to use these
hard times as fuel for my own *dream fire*. Nothing was going to hold
me back from pursuing my goals. Bad things would—and did—
happen along the way. But when they did, I'd throw another log
on my dream fire.

This same idea, I would later find out, and you will find out in
this book, is also used by Navy SEALs. Navy SEALs welcome
adversity and challenges. A SEAL knows that keeping a positive
mental attitude at the worst of times is a powerful tool that helps
you to accomplish great things. Adversity is actually an opportunity to learn and grow as a person. If you can recognize this at a
young age, it will be easier to make your dreams a reality.

Kids who don't see this often wind up making bad choices, like
doing drugs or hanging out with the wrong crowd. The same crowd
may look cool from the outside, but it's all fake. Most of these kids
are really insecure on the inside. And, as you will learn from this
book, what's on the inside is what counts most.

I have wanted to be a Navy SEAL since I was fourteen years
old. So many kids my age and adults told me this was impossible. I
call these negative people *dream stealers*. Watch out for them. Notice them for who they are, and just let whatever they say stoke your
dream fire a little more.

There were more than 220 candidates in my SEAL training
class when it began. At the end, only twenty-three of the original
candidates (me included) had made it all the way through. Roughly
90 percent of my class had failed. The best athlete in the class was
the first to quit because he didn't like getting yelled at and being
cold. He couldn't see the finish line and realize that the tough SEAL
training would eventually be over. So, when life is hard, remember
that the tough times will eventually end. And remember, too, that
the best things in life take hard work and determination to complete. Think about this next time you're practicing music, working
on math, playing sports, or doing anything else.

I was an average kid and I liked sports, but I was never the best on the team. When I entered Navy SEAL training I thought that the odds were stacked against me because of all the challenges and tough times I'd had as a kid. In reality, they were stacked in my favor. All those hard times had prepared me to pursue and realize my dreams, and complete the toughest military training in the world.

I remember a ski and snowboard trip I took with my kids in Lake Tahoe, Nevada. We had such a fun week on the mountain that none of us wanted it to end. When it did, my daughter said she couldn't believe the week had gone by so fast. I told her and my two boys that life is just like a fun week that flies by. It's over before you know it. The lesson is: Pursue your passions.

I hope you enjoy reading this book and that you will think to refer to it if you are ever down and having a tough time. You can consider it your own secret weapon to help you to pursue your ultimate dreams.

The only easy day was yesterday.

—U.S. NAVY SEALS
BRANDON WEBB

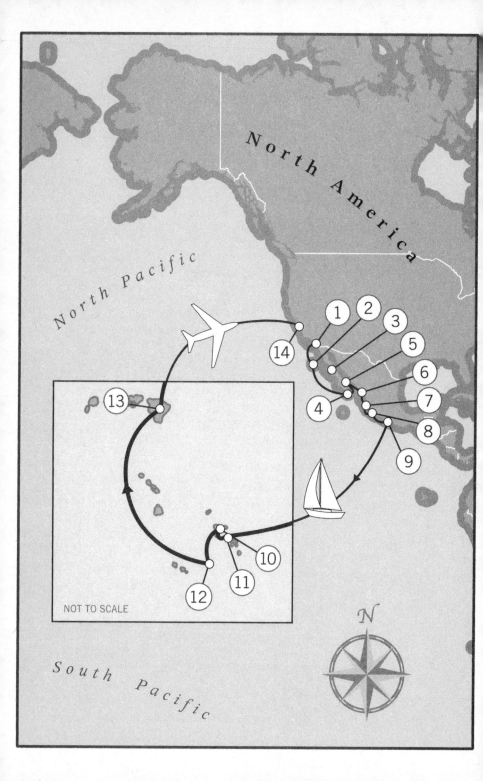

BRANDON'S FAMILY TRIP

1 San Diego, U.S.A.
2 Guadalupe Island, Mexico
3 Baja, Mexico
4 Cabo San Lucas, Mexico
5 La Paz, Mexico
6 Mazatlán, Mexico
7 Puerto Vallarta, Mexico
8 Manzanillo, Mexico
9 Acapulco, Mexico
10 Hiva Oa, Marquesas Islands
11 Nuku Hiva, Marquesas Islands
12 Papeete, Tahiti

BRANDON ON HIS OWN

13 Hilo, Hawaii
14 Ventura, California

0 Miles   2,000   4,000   6,000

0 Kilometers   4,000   6,000   10,000

PART ONE

BORN READY FOR ACTION

CHAPTER ONE

A few weeks past my sixteenth birthday, my dad threw me off a boat in the middle of the Pacific Ocean. I had to find my own way after that.

As for my father, he had been thrown out at age sixteen by his father, too. I suppose the best way to make sense out of my story is to start with his.

Jack Webb grew up in Toronto, Canada. He was short, strong, and stocky. A talented hockey player and drummer, he was always a bit of a wild man. Jack grew his hair long and also had a full black beard as soon as he was old enough to grow one. His father threatened to kick Jack out if he didn't shave the beard off and cut his long hair. My father refused, and out he went.

Suddenly on his own, Jack made his way from Toronto to Malibu, California, where he managed to get landscaping jobs. Soon he had his own company. Driving home from a job one day, he picked up three hitchhikers. One of them, named Lynn, became his wife—and, eventually, my mother.

After they got married, my parents moved up to British Columbia, Canada, to a little ski town called Kimberley. There, my dad took a job as a guide at a hunting lodge, even though he knew absolutely nothing about hunting. The guy who hired him said, "Stay on the trail, and you'll be fine." He was. His first time out, he took a small group into the Canadian Rockies, where he pointed out all sorts of wildlife. When they got back, the group told my dad's boss he'd hired the greatest guide in the world. They didn't know he was just winging it.

Soon Jack was working construction. He taught himself everything there was to know about building houses. In those days, if you were a builder you did it all—pouring foundation, framing, wiring, installing drywall, plumbing, roofing, everything from A to Z. Jack had never graduated high school, but he had a big appetite for learning. He quickly became an accomplished builder with his own company.

This is when I came into the picture. I was born on June 12, 1974, screaming at the top of my tiny lungs. According to my mom, I screamed for weeks. For the next ten months I apparently stayed awake every night yelling my head off until seven in the morning. At that point, I would sleep blissfully through the day while my mom recovered from a sleepless night. My parents did everything they could to keep me awake during the day so I would sleep at night, but it didn't happen.

According to my mom, I was as wild as the Canadian landscape. I started crawling at six months—and crawled everywhere. My mom had heard of a study where they put babies on a glass counter to see how far they would crawl. Nearly all the babies stopped when they got close to the edge—about one percent went crawling off into thin air. "That one percent?" she tells people. "That was Brandon."

I started walking at nine months, and, after that, there was not a gate or door that could hold me. My mom bought every childproof lock she could find. However, "childproof" did not mean

"Brandon-proof." She had doorknobs that she couldn't open, but I could. She would strap me into my high chair, but if she turned her back for just a moment, I'd be gone.

By eighteen months I had discovered the joys of climbing. I could climb up, over, into, and out of pretty much anything. This ability, combined with my easy friendship with locks and my tendency to drink anything I could get my hands on, added up to quite a few visits to the emergency room. I needed to have my little toddler-sized stomach pumped many times after I sampled things I didn't know I shouldn't drink, like kerosene, bleach, and Avon honeysuckle after-bath splash. By the time I was three, the hospital emergency room staff and my mom knew each other on a first-name basis.

When my mom was pregnant with my sister, Maryke, my dad built a gated enclosure with a swing in it. To this day, my mom still doesn't know how I did it—since she was sitting right there reading a book—but I got out of the enclosure, scooted down a steep hill, and disappeared before she realized I was gone. My mother was wild with fear. Just the night before, she and my father had seen a pack of coyotes ranging around. Now, all she could think about was how her tiny son would make a tasty little coyote meal. She managed to spot me because I was wearing a red sweatshirt. Somehow she coaxed me back up the hill and under the fence. Then she grabbed me, crying hysterically.

My parents quickly figured out that while they couldn't control my wild energy, they could channel it. Once they saw how much I loved skiing, they knew they'd stumbled on a parenting strategy that would serve us all well for years to come. To try to keep me out of trouble, they would get me involved in every sports activity possible. It worked, too—at least for a while.

By age five I was on a ski team. Some of my earliest memories are of the crisp cold air in my face and the schuss sound of the snow under my skis as I flew down a 2,500-foot hill. Every day during ski season, my mom would pick me up from kindergarten and drive to the slopes. We had a season skiing pass, and we used it to the max.

At the time, this hill seemed to be an enormous mountain in an endless world of snow and adventure. I can clearly remember spending countless afternoons on my bright, yellow Mickey Mouse K2 skis, exploring every trail and out-of-the-way patch.

My best friend at the time was a kid named Justin. We spent every afternoon we could exploring that hill together. Justin and I got into ski racing and joined a team. By the time we were in first grade, our team was competing in tournaments. My mom still has some first-place ribbons I took at the age of six.

By age seven I had also piled wrestling, football, baseball, swimming, and track onto my athletic schedule.

While all these sports kept me occupied, I still found time to get into trouble. My dad was usually in charge of my punishment. I was not exactly scared of him, but I knew my dad was in charge. He was not afraid to whip out his belt and get after me when he thought I needed it. Over the years, my backside and my dad's leather belt really got to know each other. Now that I'm a parent myself, I believe in discipline just as much as my dad did. But instead of getting a spanking, my kids do push-ups. My son can knock out more push-ups than most adults I know.

Although my dad was very strict, he was also not afraid to hug me and tell me he loved me. He was a good father, and I have a lot of happy memories of him from those early years.

When my dad went out to a construction job site, he often took me with him. I loved it. It always felt like an adventure, just me and my dad going to these serious grown-up work sites. My dad was also captain of his hockey team, and I would go with him when they would play. These games were typically pretty late at night, because the players all had full-time jobs.

Even though I was only five, no matter how late it was, I never got tired at my dad's hockey games. I would go through the place and look for lost pucks. I'd look for quarters, too, so I could play the big, brand-new Atari Asteroids video game they had there. Crawling around, exploring every inch of the place, it felt a lot like being up on the mountain. In a way this was even better, though, because I got to be with my dad. After practice we hung out in the locker room. I thought it was the coolest thing ever, being surrounded by sweaty hockey players who were cursing, laughing, and cracking beers. I could tell my dad really enjoyed having me there too.

I looked up to Dad. In many ways, he was my hero. Then, about the time I turned six, our lives changed.

CHAPTER TWO

My father had always been into sailing. Both my parents had a dream of sailing around the world someday. And in 1980, when I turned six, business was doing so well they decided it was time to take a few years off and turn that dream into a reality. We owned a beautiful sixty-foot Sparkman & Stephens ketch. Why not let that become our new home as we circled the globe?

Just as we were getting ready to leave, my dad decided to do one more big construction project. This last gig, he said, would really set us up well financially. A group of investors was going to pay for everything once the place was built. So my dad took out a large construction loan and built the place. But then the economy slumped and my dad wound up with no investors—and the bill for the whole thing. He negotiated with the bank to work out a way to repay the loan. But after two years my dad had to declare bankruptcy. We lost everything, including our own home.

Being so young at the time, I didn't quite grasp what

was happening. Nobody ever sat me down and said, "Brandon, we're ruined, wiped out." Even so, I could feel something was really wrong.

I remember going into the bank one day with my dad to close our accounts—the same bank he'd been wrestling with for the past year—because we were about to move away from Kimberley. One of these was a savings account he had opened for me some two years earlier.

It had been a big deal for both of us when we opened it. "Look, Brandon," I remember him telling me, "this is your first savings account. We're opening it in your name—this is going to be your money." He showed me the passbook and the first line, where he had entered the first deposit. "Now you get to watch it grow." I was so excited, and I could tell he was too.

Now my dad was informed it had a zero balance.

"What?" he practically shouted at the teller. He was furious. "How is that possible?"

I don't remember how much was in there. I knew it wasn't much, but monthly fees had apparently wiped out whatever it was, without my dad even realizing it. My dad had wanted to teach me a life lesson about how you can invest and save. The only lesson I learned that day was that you can get wiped out without even realizing it.

When I was seven we left Canada for good. We moved to a little town called Blaine, in Washington State. There, we began the painful process of starting over.

I began to realize that something pretty serious was going on. We were in a strange place in a smaller house. When my mom took me shopping for new school clothes, we hit the thrift shops instead of the big department stores. We weren't just living in a different place. Our lives were completely different.

My dad was different too. He was moodier and angrier, and tougher on me. The whole thing had devastated him. Today, more than thirty years later, he is still getting over it, and I can't say I blame him. As a kid, though, I didn't understand any of that. All I knew was that before, I would go everywhere with him. Now I didn't see him much. I have always loved my dad, but I think, during these years, a wedge started quietly growing between us.

It was in Blaine that I started fighting with other kids and acting out in all sorts of ways. My parents quickly got me as involved in sports as they could.

What I remember most about Blaine is baseball and wrestling. I was crazy about wrestling. It was also one of the few ways I could regularly connect with my dad. My dad came to all the matches to cheer our team on. I also loved going on trips with the team to compete in matches. In fourth grade I placed second in the regionals and made it to the state championships. I could tell my dad was proud of me.

Another thing that made life in Blaine better was making new friends. I had three especially good buddies there: Chris Bysh, Gaytor Rasmussen, and Scott Dodd. We are all in touch to this day. Chris became my best friend and we did lots of sports together, especially baseball.

On our Little League team, Chris played catcher and I was the pitcher. We did well enough to make it to All-Stars. We even got invited to attend a special, summer baseball camp being hosted by the Baltimore Orioles. I was so excited. It was going to be a blast!

It never happened. Instead my parents shipped Maryke and me off to Toronto to stay with relatives for the whole summer. It was my dad's idea. I was absolutely furious. What was wrong with him? I could not believe he was going to take away this incredible opportunity and ruin my summer, for no good reason whatsoever!

He actually had a very good reason. It was just one he couldn't tell us. At the time, my parents' marriage was on rocky ground. They wanted to make a serious attempt to save it. They thought they would have a better shot at it if they didn't have to tiptoe around Maryke and me for a few months. But of course, I didn't know any of that until many years later.

My father also started picking up the pieces of his career. He found a job as the foreman of a large construction company and was soon building houses again. He and my mom had never given up on their dream of sailing around the world, and by the time I entered fifth grade we were able to purchase another boat to replace the one we had lost when we had gone bankrupt.

Soon after we got the boat, we left Blaine and moved a hundred miles or so south, to Seattle. We now lived on the boat, which we christened *Agio*, which is an Italian word that means "ease." There were times when life on the *Agio* lived up to its name. And there were times when it most definitely did not.

My parents were excited about the move and hopeful about the future. Me, not so much. We had moved a lot since I was a baby, and I was starting to seriously resent it. It seemed like as soon as I made some new friends and started to settle into a place, we'd up and move. Then I'd have to go through the whole thing all over again. Looking back on this time, I can see how the ability to adapt to new circumstances probably served to build character in both Maryke and me. At the time, though, it just felt hard. I was jealous of kids who got to stay in one town and have the friends they'd known since preschool.

After a few years in Seattle, we pulled up stakes and moved yet again, this time sailing down the coast to Ventura, California. To me, it felt like the weather during the move reflected my bad mood. We hit the tail end of a hurricane a hundred miles off the coast of Oregon. For more than twenty-four hours we struggled with the full brunt of nature's gale-force winds. Finally, my father dropped our sails and put out a sea anchor. We waited for the storm to pass.

The next few dozen hours left a deep impression on me. I remember my mother gripping Maryke and me close to her, life jackets donned and survival raft at the ready, wondering which would have more staying power—us on our boat, or the hurricane. In the end, after nearly two days, the storm must have decided we were not worth it. It finally released its grip and moved on. We found we had been pushed almost two hundred miles in the wrong direction.

When we finally pulled into land, at Coos Bay, Oregon, a crowd of locals had gathered on the docks. They wanted to meet the family they heard had been out there on the ocean's angry face and survived the storm. Everyone loves a good sea story.

CHAPTER THREE

We finally made it all the way to Ventura, California. I was ten when we got there.

We would live on the *Agio* for the better part of the next six years. While we each had our own stateroom, it was still tight quarters, and I looked for every opportunity to escape.

My life in California revolved around the water. All my new friends surfed, and I soon joined them. I also started getting into trouble again. My mom, who went to work for a few years on California's offshore oil platforms, never knew what to expect when she came home. Once she found me and some friends hunting squirrels with homemade blowguns. Another time she saw the boat's mast swaying from a distance. She broke into a run. When she reached the boat she saw that my friends and I were taking turns pushing off and swinging around the mast on a harness I'd rigged.

During most of this time, my father and I might as well have been living on separate planets. He was working round the clock. He would leave early in the morning and come back at five—briefly—for dinner.

There was a period there, though, when I was in eighth grade, when my dad made an extra effort to get me into ice hockey. The closest rink was in Thousand Oaks, nearly an hour's drive away. During hockey season he would get up every Saturday at 5:30 A.M. to drive me out there for practice. He even helped coach the team. Throughout that hockey season the two of us had an opportunity to bond again. That soon came abruptly to an end, and my sports career with it.

I'd noticed that my knees were starting to ache, and toward the end of that hockey season it got pretty severe. I could play through it, but after practice I had a swollen bump on each knee. If you tapped a particular spot, it felt like someone was jamming an ice pick into my knee.

My folks took me to the doctor, and he knew what it was right away. "Your boy has Osgood-Schlatter syndrome," he said. "He's been involved in sports so constantly and for so long, his knees haven't had the chance to develop properly."

He told us that in rare cases surgery was needed. He didn't think that would be necessary for me. But I would have to wear a brace for a while.

"Of course," he added, "he'll have to cut out all sports."

My mom nearly gasped. She said, "What do you mean, cut out all sports?" She was terrified. Without sports, she knew I would just get into worse and worse trouble.

First, they put my legs in braces. As soon as the braces were on, I was off skateboarding around the harbor. Finally they realized they had no choice but to put me in casts. As much as I hated them, those casts probably saved my life, or at least my knees. Confined to plaster casts, my joints were finally able to grow properly. I've never had knee problems since.

At the time, it was also a disaster of sorts. I was a freshman in high school, and I desperately wanted to wrestle and play baseball. No dice. I spent my ninth-grade year with casts on my legs. As soon as they were off, though, so was I—off getting into trouble again.

Then my mother had a new idea. If I couldn't play sports to keep me busy, I could get a job. Soon before my thirteenth birthday, she introduced me to a man named Bill Magee. Bill owned a charter dive boat called the *Peace*. He offered to let me work on the boat.

I worked on the *Peace* all summer, every summer, for the next few years. Everything about being on that dive boat, with the tantalizing possibility of adventure outside Ventura Harbor, completely captivated me. It's no exaggeration to say that going to work on the *Peace* changed the course of my life.

Bill Magee was one of the nicest men I've ever known. He and the boat's captain, Michael Roach, were like second fathers to me. They watched out for me and trusted me with a lot of responsibility. I had not had that kind of experience before. They showed me a whole new side to the concept of respect, and instilled in me the belief that I could be somebody and do something special with my life.

Bill had made some money in construction and eventually sold a successful roofing company up in the Bay Area, which had allowed him to buy the *Peace*.

Captain Roach was the classic salty Irish sea captain. He taught me how to give a firm handshake and look a man straight in the eye when you were talking to him.

Strictly speaking, the *Peace* was a dive boat, which meant that people paid to be taken out scuba diving. Unofficially, it was also a party boat. We'd take passengers out diving during the day. When we were anchored up for the night, we would party. Bill would front me a few hundred dollars so I could sit down and join the poker games. Here I was, at thirteen, playing poker with the guys.

At the same time, the work was no joke. When you weren't on an anchor watch, it was fine to whoop it up and party, but when you were on, you had to be on. You had to know your limits and your abilities. I didn't know it at the time, but this experience was great preparation for becoming a Navy SEAL.

As the most junior guy on the *Peace*, I often got assigned the chores nobody else wanted to do. One of these was diving down to free the anchor if it got stuck when we were ready to move. This often happened in the middle of the night. I'd be rousted out of a deep sleep to dive down into the dark water with a flashlight. It was one way to get over a fear of the dark—never mind a fear of sharks. It was terrifying, and I loved it.

Working on the *Peace*, I learned to scuba dive in the open water of the Pacific Ocean right from the start. There were no pool sessions for me. Pretty soon I found I preferred diving without a buoyancy compensator, a kind of inflatable vest with an air hose plugged into it that most divers wear. I thought it was a crutch. To me, it was like the difference between swimming in a full suit of clothes and swimming in a Speedo. So I never used one. I also found I liked going down with two tanks, instead of the single tank most sport divers prefer. A second tank adds significant weight, so you have to be fit enough to handle it, but you get more bottom time and can swim serious distances. Sport divers typically just drop straight down and goof around for a while. Serious divers mean business and wear two tanks.

By my second summer on the *Peace* I had logged over two hundred dives and was equipped with twin steel 72s (72-cubic-foot-capacity scuba tanks), and no buoyancy compensator—just a single- and second-stage scuba regulator and a large spear gun.

It was Captain Mike and James Hrabak, the alternate second captain, who taught me how to stalk and hunt in the reefs and open water—skills that would prove enormously useful later on. I quickly became an accomplished hunter on tanks or free diving (just holding my breath). It didn't matter if it was yellowtail, calico bass, halibut, abalone, or lobster—I was all over it, and nothing was safe.

Usually when we took paying customers out on a dive it would be a pretty mellow thing. There was one group of hard-core divers, though, guys I thought of as the Animals, who would come out with us a few times a year. With the usual passengers, we might dive three times a day. With the Animals, we would do six serious dives every day, hunting for lobster in the winter, halibut or some other fish in the summer. These guys got the biggest kick out of seeing me surface with no buoyancy compensator, two steel tanks, and a forty-pound halibut in my bag.

Eventually I became a rescue diver and an accomplished deckhand. I was often trusted at the helm of the boat from midnight to 2:00 A.M., on a night transit to the islands. To be a teenager manning the helm of a seventy-foot dive boat with thirty-two sleeping passengers and transiting through one of the busiest shipping lanes in the world was clearly a huge responsibility. I took it very seriously and never had an incident. By the time I was approaching my sixteenth birthday, I had made more than a thousand dives and had enough hours and knowledge to take the Coast Guard 100-ton Master Captain license.

The guys I worked with on that boat were really good at what they did and took their jobs seriously. Bill and Captain Mike set a standard of excellence that I would often be reminded of during my time with the Navy SEALs.

CHAPTER FOUR

At the close of my freshman year at Ventura High, my parents decided the time was finally right for us to embark on our world-encircling sailing trip on the *Agio*. They had saved enough money, and they knew that the longer they put it off, the older Maryke and I would be. They figured, better do it while we were still young enough to go along with the plan.

Still, whenever they would talk about this voyage, I would ignore it and hope the whole idea would go away. I was having a great time working on the *Peace* and enjoying the incredible freedom of my harbor lifestyle. Sailing off to faraway places with my family didn't sound thrilling. I had more important things to do—like diving, surfing, chasing girls, and getting my driver's license.

I didn't know it at the time, but Captain Bill talked to my parents and offered to let me stay with him on the *Peace* when they left. They apparently appreciated the offer, but said no. They decided we were going to make this trip all together as a family. They put Maryke and me on independent studies for a year.

Our first stop was San Diego Harbor to stock up on supplies. Then we headed down to Guadalupe Island and Cabo San Lucas in Mexico. After a few weeks in Cabo, we sailed around the tip of Baja into La Paz. Then we spent a few weeks in and around the surrounding islands before heading over to mainland Mexico. We hit Mazatlán, Puerto Vallarta, Manzanillo, and finally Acapulco, our last point to resupply before leaving the continent behind. Soon we headed southwest, traversing thousands of miles of open water into the heart of the South Pacific, bound for the sparsely populated Marquesas Islands, not far from Tahiti. It took us a month to get there.

Thirty days doesn't sound like a lot, but when you're out on the open sea with nothing but water, it is an eternity. My sister and I did have some good times, though. We sat up on the bow and watched the dolphins jump and play in our boat's bow wake. We also always had a line out and caught quite a few fish.

My dad and I split the night watch between us. I would take over from my mom and sister at midnight, watch from then until 4:00 A.M., and then hand it off to my father, who took it till sunrise. The night sky over the South Pacific was amazing. There were times when the sky was so clear and filled with stars it felt like we were floating in space. Every ten minutes or so, I would see a shooting star.

These periods of solitude, with the heavens opened up like the pages of a book before me, began working on my mind. During those long hours I started reflecting on my life, on all the experiences I'd had, and I could not help but think about the future.

I think this is something most kids never have the chance to experience, this kind of break in the day when there is nothing to think about but the expanse of time and the possibilities it holds. While my family and I were crossing the South Pacific, all my friends were back at school, running around, going to class, chasing girls, going to sleep, and then waking up and doing it all over again the next day. Their lives were full of distractions and commotion, with little time for genuine introspection.

I can't say I came to any startling new self-knowledge during this time, but in some way I couldn't have explained, it felt like my thinking sank a little deeper, and maybe grew bigger. I began to get the sense that I wanted to do something different—something special—with my life. I didn't know exactly what that might be, but I knew that as much as I loved the life of a dive boat captain, which is what Bill Magee and Captain Mike had been grooming me for during the last few years, I would never be content with the harbor. There was an impatience growing inside me, an urge that was starting to whisper, *Wherever my life is heading, let's get on with it!*

Those thirty days at sea also provided the time to accomplish a lot. I finished my entire school year (months ahead of schedule), taught myself how to juggle, and read a ton of books. I went through the entire Lord of the Rings series and a carton full of classic novels.

I also practiced celestial navigation, using the sky as a guide, with my dad. This was in the days before the GPS existed. We had a satellite navigation unit, but it took a wait of twelve hours for a satellite to get overhead for us to fix our position that way. So we did a lot of navigation the old-fashioned way: through looking at the sky and through dead reckoning.

After thirty days we made landfall at Hiva Oa, one of the Marquesas Islands. Shrouded in a nearly constant cloud cover, the Marquesas rise majestically out of the Pacific. The local harbor is a thing of beauty with its gorgeous black sand beaches and waterfalls high up on the distant cliffs.

We anchored the *Agio* in a cove and took a small boat ashore. The lifestyle of the people we encountered was both amazing and hilarious to me. They lived in fairly primitive, thatched-roof huts— and drove brand-new Toyota four-wheel drives, paid for in part by the government.

On Hiva Oa I met a girl I will never forget. I never knew her name; there was a complete language barrier between us. Somehow, though, we just clicked. We took long walks through the most stunning tropical scenery, past the most amazing waterfalls, and as beautiful as our surroundings were, she was even more so. She was something out of a dream. I never even kissed her, but after we left, I missed her badly. Of course, I knew we couldn't stay and that it wasn't my dad's fault we had to leave, but still, I hated it.

Up to this point in our trip, my dad and I had been having a steadily escalating series of disagreements on points of seamanship. So far these had been fairly minor—but things were about to change.

On the open ocean it wasn't that bad. When you're sailing straight in one direction, all you're really doing is taking fixes and monitoring your course. Every time we'd get closer in to land, though, and especially when it came to navigating the coastal waterways, the two of us would start to butt heads. I wanted more of a say in how we managed the boat. I felt like I should be consulted. By this time I'd had a lot of experience in coastal waterway navigation. "I'm no slouch," I'd say. "I know what I'm doing here."

In the South Pacific, because of the nature of the deepwater reefs, it's common to set two anchors. First you set a bow hook off the front, and then you throw a stern anchor off the back and snug the boat up tight. For both anchors, my father was using a type of anchor called a CQR that he'd used for most of his boating life. A CQR is a plow type of anchor that does an excellent job of holding in sand, clay, or mud bottoms. It's just not the best choice to hold in rocks or coral reef, which is the kind of seafloor we had here.

We also had a multipurpose Bruce anchor on board that I had salvaged from my time on the dive boat. The Bruce is designed to function in a wide range of seafloor compositions. Because of its fierce reliability, it is the choice of most commercial boats. The Bruce and I knew each other well, going back to my early days working on the dive boat. In fact, it was the reason for many of those 2:00 A.M. wake-up calls. That Bruce anchor would hold fast in anything. It was the anchor I favored.

"Look," I said, "we're in a coral reef. I get what the underwater topography looks like here, Dad, I'm a diver. Do you have any idea how many stuck anchors I've dealt with? Trust me, we need the Bruce on the bow."

My father didn't see it that way. "There's only one captain on this boat" was all he'd say. "And you know who that is."

I was so frustrated. At the same time, I was being a wise guy with a bad attitude about the whole thing. My parents couldn't stop me from screaming my head off when I was two weeks old, and at sixteen I guess I hadn't gotten much easier to persuade to shut up.

That first night in port we set our bow and rear anchors, again both CQRs. Of the two, the bow is the more important. When we awoke the next morning I was delighted to see that we had dragged the bow anchor right along the ocean floor and nearly grounded our boat. I couldn't wait to give my dad an earful about how useless that CQR was. Equally well spelled out was this: I was being obnoxious.

Every time we argued, my sister would go to her room to get away from the tension, while my mom would try to be the peacemaker. Of course, she would side with my dad, but then later on she would come to my stateroom privately, sit down with me, and say, "Brandon, you have to chill out. I know you have a lot of experience, but this is your dad's boat." I would vent my frustration to her, and she would be understanding and try to keep the situation from spiraling out of control. For a while, she succeeded.

Our trip continued on through the rest of the island chain to the Marquesas' main northern island, Nuku Hiva, and then on to the Tuamotu Archipelago, a series of coral atolls that comprise the largest atoll chain in the world. All the while, my father and I kept arguing. By the time we pulled into Papeete, the capital of Tahiti, the situation between us had badly deteriorated.

I don't remember what I said that finally set him off, but whatever it was, it brought an end not only to my trip with my family but also my life with my family. Suddenly my dad had me by the scruff of the neck, his fist curled and ready to lash out, both of us screaming at each other. He didn't hit me, but we both knew we'd reached a point of no return. One of us had to go—and it wasn't going to be him. With my mom and sister wailing in grief and disbelief, my father threw me off the boat.

He didn't actually hurl me off physically. He just told me that I should take a pack with me and find passage aboard another boat to my destination of choice. He said it like he meant it.

Before I knew it I was off the *Agio* for good—and on my own in the middle of the South Pacific.

CHAPTER FIVE

In a way, I was relieved. The tension between us had grown unbearable. I knew that if we didn't part ways, something really bad would happen that would cause irreparable harm to our relationship. In a way, I also didn't blame my father for throwing me off the boat. It felt like the only possible thing to do. Still, I was somewhat in shock. I was also scared.

My mom was completely torn up and pleaded and pleaded with him to relent, and yet I think that she also realized that there was no going back. She knew that if I could make my way home, Bill Magee would take me in. So, before I left Tahiti, she helped me get a radio call patched through to him so we could fill him in. She also helped me secure passage on the *Shilo*, a forty-foot catamaran headed for Hilo, Hawaii, a journey of nearly 3,000 miles. My boat mates were a couple and their three-year-old son. The mom's hands were pretty full taking care of their son, and they had been looking for crew.

I stood the midnight shift on the *Shilo*, which left

me plenty of time to think about the future. During the day, I was either asleep or occupied with the practical matters of the boat. During the nights, I was alone with my thoughts. Those nights were rough. My whole family was gone. Those first few nights on that forty-foot cat, I cried myself to sleep.

When I could finally get past being scared, I found there was also a part of me that was excited about whatever lay ahead. I knew my life had hit a major turning point. I'd had experiences most other sixteen-year-olds wouldn't have dreamed of. Still, I was far from being an adult. I didn't even have my driver's license.

Often, during those lonely nights, I thought about what had happened with my dad and me back in the harbor off Papeete. On the one hand, it was a hard lesson in the demands of authority. My dad was right: there's only one captain on a ship, just like there's only one person in charge of a mission, or a department, or almost any venture. At the same time, he was making the wrong decision. I had learned how to take orders during my time on the *Peace*, and that sense of respect for the chain of command served me well, especially later on during my military service. But I also always had a need to speak up and challenge authority whenever my gut told me the guy in charge was leading me down the wrong path.

That catamaran was fast—way faster than any boat with a single hull I'd ever sailed. It took us less than two weeks to make Hilo.

A day before we got there, I came up on deck from my stateroom on the port side of the boat. It was a gorgeous morning. As I stood on deck, something in the hull caught my eye. I bent down to look. Just above the waterline, a swordfish had rammed our boat during the night, spearing himself straight through the hull and breaking off the tip of his snout. That fish must have leapt clear out of the water to spear us. I grabbed my camera to take a picture of it. I still have that snapshot. The next day we breezed into the harbor at Hilo with a short length of swordfish beak jammed through our hull.

The image of that swordfish stuck in my mind as firmly as its beak stuck in the *Shilo*'s flank. What was going on with that fish? What made it leap up out of the water to attack this strange, unknown vessel? Did it know it was going up against something more than ten times larger and heavier than itself?

What future was I leaping out of the water to go up against?

Years later I would learn this odd factoid of biology: Although like all fish it is cold-blooded, the swordfish has special organs in its head that heat the eyes and brain as much as 60°F above the surrounding temperature. This greatly enhances the animal's vision and therefore its ability to nail its prey. The falcon or eagle would probably be most people's choice, but if you were looking for an animal to represent the idea of a sniper—especially a sniper who works in water—the swordfish would not be a bad pick.

Once we reached Hilo I made my way back to the mainland by plane and met up with Bill Magee. As my mom had predicted, Bill was happy to see me and said I could go back to work for him and live on board. "Hey," he said, "you've already got your schoolwork out of the way for the rest of the year. Why don't you just settle into boat life?"

I can't even imagine how my life might have turned out if he hadn't made this kind offer.

Soon after I rejoined Captain Bill and the *Peace*, the Animals showed up for a few days of diving. This time one of them, a younger guy, brought a few friends with him. These guys were rugged. I didn't know what they did, but you could see that whatever it was, they knew it inside and out. They weren't muscle-bound showoffs or tough guys with attitude, it was more subtle than that. Being around them, you could just sense that there was something special about the way these guys carried themselves. It felt like they could take on a shark on a bad day and come out smiling.

On our first dive, when these guys saw me, a sixteen-year-old kid diving with no buoyancy compensator and my twin steel 72s, they noticed. "Who is this kid?" one of them asked.

The two of us got to talking. He wanted to know how I'd come to be a deckhand, and I told him a little bit about my background. "You know," he said, "you should check out the seals."

At least that's what I thought he said. I had no idea what he was talking about. Seals? Was this guy seriously into seals, like whale watching? Was he making a joke?

"No," he said, "not seals—SEALs."

I still didn't get it.

"Navy maritime special operations forces," he explained. "SEALs. It stands for sea, air, and land. SEALs."

I'd never heard of them before.

"To become a SEAL," he added, "you go through the toughest military training in the world."

Now, that got my attention. I didn't know much about the military, but I had always been fascinated with aviation and had thought about becoming a pilot when I grew up. Maybe even an astronaut. What he was describing, though, really intrigued me. I love the water, I thought, and I'm a pretty good diver. That sounds like it could be the right challenge for me.

The truth was, I knew I needed a plan, somewhere to go and something to aim for. From that point on, my goal was fixed: I was going to become a Navy SEAL.

I had no idea how hard it would be.

PART TWO

BOOT CAMP TRAINING

CHAPTER SIX

It was March 1993. I was nineteen years old and about to enter navy boot camp in Orlando, Florida.

At the airport, a few other boot camp candidates and I were met by the local navy representative, who put us on a bus. It took about forty minutes to reach the U.S. Naval Training Center. Most of those minutes passed in a silence filled with excitement—and dread.

As we pulled into the training center, we saw a few dozen guys lining the roadway, yelling obscenities at us. Our welcome committee. It felt like we were in a bad prison movie.

It was ten o'clock at night. We just had time to unload, find out where we were supposed to bunk, and hit the sack. I heard a few of my bus mates cry themselves to sleep that first night. That didn't bother me. What I really didn't appreciate was the 4:00 A.M. wake-up call the next morning with some senior recruits banging on aluminum trash cans and yelling at us to wake up.

I've been a physically active person all my life, and

I thought of myself as being in pretty good shape. Ha. Boot camp taught me otherwise. Doing the physical training (PTs) was one thing: push-ups and more push-ups. But what really got to us all were the endless hours of marching drills.

Picture one hundred new recruits—that's the number in each company—from all over the country, all walks of life, and all levels of preparedness. Now picture us having to learn how to walk in step, pivot and turn, march right, march left, pivot and turn. Every time anyone messed up—which was practically every second of every minute of every hour—we would be ordered to drop to the pavement, hot and sweating, and push out another ten or another twenty push-ups. Then we were back on our feet to get it right. Which, of course, we didn't.

It was grueling. Any chance we could grab to lie down flat on the concrete and rest, even for just half a minute, felt like heaven. When night came, I was dog-tired. And I was one of the better prepared people there.

Soon after we arrived in Orlando, they gathered us all in a big circle and went around asking each of us in turn, "What do you want to do in the navy?"

When my turn came, I didn't have to think about it. "I want to be a SEAL," I said.

I knew what reaction to expect, and was not surprised when it came. "Good luck with that," one guy sneered. Snickers and wisecracks rippled around the circle.

Like I mentioned earlier, it has always amazed me that, whenever you tell people about something big you want to accomplish, many of them will try to shoot it down. I think they don't even realize they're doing it. Often there's no evil intent. It's just the reaction people have when you state big goals. Maybe they're threatened by you and your dreams. Maybe by undercutting your goals, they get to justify their own insecurities and self-doubts.

Maybe they're just plain negative. To tell the truth, I don't know what their reasons are. And I don't really want to know.

This had been happening for three years, ever since I'd first set my sights on becoming a Navy SEAL. Every now and then someone would say, "Wow, that's great, you'd be awesome at that." But not very often. Usually, when I told anyone, whether it was a teacher, an acquaintance, or even a friend, what I got back was disbelief and ridicule. Now that I was in the navy, it only got worse. Everyone here knew that the SEALs have one of the hardest training programs in the world.

For me this was just fuel for the fire. The more I heard it, the more that fire was stoked. I knew the only way I'd be able to prove I was serious was to ignore the critics and just do it.

CHAPTER SEVEN

A few weeks into boot camp, the SEAL recruiter came around. He showed us a brief video that described the life of a SEAL. We saw guys being tested underwater, shivering in the cold, going through the various trials of BUD/S (Basic Underwater Demolition/SEAL).

After the video ended, I went up to the guy and asked him where I should sign up. He shot me a look that said, *It's not gonna be that easy*. Understatement of the decade.

Four other guys were also interested. The recruiter explained to us that we needed to muster at 4:45 the next morning to begin our physical and mental conditioning. That was an hour earlier than we were already getting up. I wasn't looking forward to it—but hey, if that was the price of admission, I was glad to pay it.

The next morning, it was just me and two of the other four guys. Those two no-shows were the first of hundreds of guys I would see fall by the wayside on my journey to becoming a SEAL.

Throughout the rest of basic training, the three of us got up an hour earlier than everyone else, to get in shape for BUD/S. I was fired up about it. This was what I was here for. But man, those PTs were killer.

It was a hundred push-ups just to warm up. Then a thousand flutter kicks. You lie on your back, hands under you, and scissor-kick your legs in the air. Murder on the abdominals. Try one. Then think about doing one thousand of them. Every day.

After that, pull-ups—dozens, then dozens more, then dozens more. This hour was brutal, but it got me into shape.

Before long, the three of us became two.

As the weeks went by and we drew closer to graduation, I kept asking about my orders to BUD/S. I finally got a SEAL to look into the situation for me. I found out that my path to BUD/S was taking a detour.

"Sorry, Webb," the SEAL told me. "You have orders to Search and Rescue [SAR]—and they're undermanned. We can't just yank you out. You'll have to wait until you get to your final duty station and then apply for a transfer."

I pleaded with him to let me switch programs, but there was little he could do for me. It turns out that when, fresh out of high school, back in California, I had first signed up for the navy, the placement officer told me that going into the Naval Air Crew Candidate School (NACCS) and SAR was the best way to get to BUD/S. So I had put that down. It turns out he was wrong.

"Be patient," the SEAL advised me. "You're showing promise. Keep at it."

I would keep at it—for the next four years. That detour on the way to BUD/S was a long one.

CHAPTER EIGHT

My dad showed up in Orlando for my graduation from boot camp, and I could tell he was proud of me.

When he first heard I was serious about the navy, my dad was there for me, cheering me along. He even gave me a Ford Ranger as a combined high-school-graduation/ congratulations-for-enlisting-in-the-navy gift. While so many other people were dumping on my dreams of becoming a SEAL, my dad had been totally supportive. Given our rocky history together, this had felt especially good.

Things had not gone well for my parents' marriage. After returning from that ill-fated boat trip (minus one teenaged son), they had found themselves faced with too many differences and unable to work things out. My dad decided to move out.

My mom was crushed, but in time managed to get past it, if not entirely over it. Eventually she met another guy. Within a few years my dad must have realized what he'd lost, because suddenly he was trying to win her back. But it was a one-way bridge he'd driven her over. She wasn't going back.

Every now and then he would come visit me on the *Peace*, and do a little scuba diving. Our relationship continued to be pretty much as strained as it had been on the *Agio*. On one of these visits, soon after my seventeenth birthday, we went diving off Gull Island. We anchored up, and he was one of the first guys into the water. A half hour later he headed up toward the surface—and surfaced right smack into a big patch of kelp. It was a very bad spot, with the surf breaking over an especially rocky coast. He got tangled up in the kelp, panicked, and spit his regulator out.

At the time, I was serving as the rescue diver, so I dove in to help him. I can remember the scene as if it were happening right now: I'm staring at Jack Webb, this tough-guy hero of mine who is panicking and yelling for help—and *I'm* the one there to rescue him.

It was hard to wrap my head around, but my training kicked in. I dove into the water in a flash and pulled him out of there. It put us in a weird situation. We never talked about it, but it hovered there, making our already complicated relationship even more awkward.

A week before I started NACCS, I flew out to see my dad. He was now living in Jackson Hole, Wyoming. We had a great time skiing and just goofing off. We drove around in my Ford Ranger, which he had been keeping for me while I was going through navy training. I sensed he was trying to reach out to me. I appreciated it, even though things still felt a little strained between us.

I'd pretty much blown my whole first military paycheck on the plane tickets. That first check, for about two months of boot camp, had only been about $700. That averaged out to about ten dollars a day! I'd made better money on the dive boat when I was fourteen. I really didn't care. I was in the navy and on the road, no matter how many twists and turns it might have, to becoming a SEAL.

However, I needed to get my uniforms dry-cleaned. So I asked my dad for some cash.

He looked at me for a moment without saying a word. Then he gave me a hard time for hitting him up for money.

I stared at him, not believing what I was hearing. After all this time, after all we'd been through, he was going to make me feel guilty about *this*?

I lost it and started yelling. Before either of us knew what was happening I was sitting behind the wheel of that Ranger, bawling in anger and frustration.

Many years later I would learn that he knew he had messed up and felt truly terrible about the whole thing. At the time, though, it sure didn't show. A blanket of quiet hostility settled over us. He gave me the money. I vowed to myself that I would never ask him for anything again, ever. I left the Ranger with him and told him it was his now. I didn't want it.

Soon enough, I was out of there and on a plane headed for air crew school.

CHAPTER NINE

NACCS was much more relaxed than boot camp had been. While boot camp was all about physical conditioning, NACCS was mostly about getting used to flying during all kinds of conditions.

As part of the training, I was strapped into a flight simulator. Once they shut me in, the thing started moving, spinning at different speeds, now faster, now slower. It changed both speed and direction at unpredictable intervals. The whole time, a voice was talking to me through a speaker, walking me through various maneuvers. Clearly, the thing was designed to push us to the limits of our ability to withstand extreme changes of speed and motion without getting dizzy. We called the simulators "spin-'n'-pukes."

There wasn't as much PT at NACCS as there had been in boot camp. And what there was seemed pretty easy to me, though it was supposed to be more intense. I could feel myself starting to get out of shape. For some of the guys, though, it wasn't easy at all, and a few washed out because they couldn't meet the physical standards.

Most of our class was headed to work in air crew or other navy jobs. Only a handful of us were going on to SAR, and when it came time to graduate we were excited but also somewhat terrified. We knew our next step was going to be a good deal harder.

At SAR school, they ran a tight ship. We showed up early every morning for inspection, and our uniforms had to be perfect. From there we went to PT, followed by a three-mile conditioning run, followed by some swims, then the classroom. After that, we hit the pool for training.

It was an enormous indoor pool that simulated sea state, with the irregular swell of waves just like on the open ocean. They had huge spray machines to simulate helicopter rotor wash. There were also parachute-like devices hanging down from cranes that they used to drag us through the pool. We learned the basics of lifesaving, then moved on to more advanced techniques for rescuing downed airmen.

Imagine you are a pilot and you've had to eject from your aircraft. It's the middle of the night, and you've parachuted into rough water. You can't see a thing. You're weighed down and badly entangled in a web of parachute lines. The water is freezing cold. You need help. Well, SAR guys are the ones who jump out of helicopters and into the water to save you.

When people are plunged unexpectedly into the water, they tend to panic. So, even though you're out there to save someone's life, they tend to grab on to you and push you down. They don't mean to. They're just acting out of pure panic. Still, consciously or not, they are doing their level best to drown you. So we did a lot of "drown-proofing" to make sure we would be ready for whatever we might encounter.

There are dozens of different types of harnesses, straps, chutes, and other systems, and we had to know the procedures for every one of them. We also had to master a range of first-aid techniques, because you never know what kinds of injuries a downed pilot might have.

Near the end of the four weeks, it was final exam time. It took place in the pool.

The place was noisy and dimly lit, simulating a nighttime scene. The rotor chop simulator spray was on, the hoist equipment was up and running, and there below me was an instructor acting the part of a downed pilot flailing around in the water, on the edge of drowning.

I leapt off the platform and splashed down into the tank. I swam directly toward the "panicked victim." I couldn't see much and it was impossible to hear anything over the roar of the machinery and chop of the waves. Suddenly two huge arms wrapped around me like a steel bear trap, and we were both thrashing in the water. I knew it was simulated, but the instructor was a good actor. He was taking me down.

Parachute lines were everywhere. I knew I couldn't let myself get tangled in those ropes, but it was very difficult not to. Finally I managed to free myself from the guy's grip, wrestle him into the harness system, and get him hoisted up onto the helo.

Once he was laid out on the floor, I saw that he had a lot of simulated injuries. I had to administer the correct first aid if I wanted to pass the test.

That exam was tough. Fortunately for me, my years of experience on Captain Bill's dive boat had sharpened my water skills to a fine point, and I made it through okay. Not so for some of the others. The drown-proofing was where the most people washed out. In that frantic, darkened, noisy environment, feeling themselves being dragged down by a crazy person, they panicked. A few of our victims "drowned."

I was proud when I finished the course. I'm proud to this day to have belonged to the SAR community.

CHAPTER TEN

After SAR school it was time to pick an "A" school, where I would receive basic training for whichever specific naval job I elected to do. In the navy, your occupational specialization is referred to as your rating. Your rating is earned through "A" school. If you want to be a cook, you go to mess specialist "A" school. If you're a submarine sonar guy, you go to "A" school for sonar.

SAR swimmers were deployed on helicopters, and as far as I could see, the only job on an aircraft that didn't involve turning wrenches was what at the time was called an antisubmarine warfare operator, or AW. This is the guy who works the sonar in the back of the helicopter—and that sounded exciting to me. So, I headed for Millington, Tennessee, for four months of antisubmarine warfare and sonar operator training.

Toward the end of "A" school, I again inquired about BUD/S. Once again, I was told I'd need to wait and take up my request after arriving at my final duty station.

This would be when I deployed as part of an active helo squadron—which would not be for close to a year.

In January 1994 I reported to Helicopter Anti-Submarine Squadron Ten (HS-10), the helicopter training squadron in San Diego. There, I would learn the ropes before finally deploying as part of an operational squadron. However, there were a few more hurdles to clear first. Before you can become a pilot or rescue swimmer, or take any other job where there is significant risk of capture, you need two things. You have to have secret clearance, and you have to go to survival school.

The term "boot camp" was first used by the marines back in World War II. "Boot" is slang for "recruit." Those of us who showed up for Survival, Evasion, Resistance, and Escape (SERE) training that January had already been through many months of training. But we were still considered "boots." SERE was boot camp on steroids.

The program's aim is to equip its trainees with the skills and the grit needed to survive with dignity in the most hostile conditions of captivity. It was far and away the most intense training I'd encountered so far.

We spent a week of classroom training that included learning how to tell a captor just enough to stay alive—but not enough to give away secrets. Then we headed out into the field.

There was a simulated prisoner of war (POW) camp portion of the training. I was no longer Brandon Webb. I was now War Criminal 53.

There were two rules here, and you learned them pretty fast. "Grab your rags!" and "Eyes to ground!" The first meant grab the sides of your pants so the guards could see your hands at all times. The second was to ensure that we war criminals did not look around and gain any awareness of our surroundings that we might use to our advantage later.

I was assigned to a small concrete box, about three feet tall, though somewhat larger in width and depth (thank heavens). I crawled in and did my best to find a comfortable position. Hunching down a bit, I could just manage to sit cross-legged, sort of. I am not a tall man. Right then, I was grateful for this fact.

My bathroom was a Folgers coffee can. The box had a little canvas flap I could pull down for a little privacy when it came time to use the can.

This was my home for the next three days.

I wondered what would happen next. It wasn't that terrible being crammed into this ridiculous box, but I wanted them to haul me out and start interrogating me. *Let's get this over with,* I thought.

Nobody came.

As the hours crawled by, a sort of routine began to establish itself. People were randomly selected (at least it seemed that way to me), pulled out of their boxes, and taken away into the night. A short while later, we would hear screams. Then the music would start: bad songs, the worst, over and over. Other times it would be a recording of a little girl pleading for her daddy to come home. Whatever it was they played on the loudspeakers, it would go on for hours. When daybreak came this routine continued.

My most vivid memory of time in the camp was being crammed into another tiny box, this one of wood and no more than three feet in all dimensions. This wonderful location would be my accommodations for the next few hours while they subjected me to the interrogation portion. (Be careful what you wish for.) I've never had a problem with small spaces, but when I was stuffed into that box (yes, stuffed), my left leg started to cramp. This was the kind of cramp you can quickly relieve simply by straightening out your leg. But in that box, there was no straightening anything out. That leg cramp—and even more, my complete and utter inability to do anything about it—drove me near to insanity. It took everything I had to keep it together.

During the course of these three days we learned a lesson that has been learned the hard way by real POWs: in any prisoner-of-war situation, the goal is to survive with honor. More than a few people failed out for completely losing their cool or getting "executed" for acting out.

Three days doesn't sound like a very long time, and under normal, everyday circumstances, it's not—but under POW camp conditions, it doesn't take long to wear down a man's sanity.

After day three we were liberated from the camp and debriefed on our POW experience. We had been carefully watched the entire time. I was happy to find out I did pretty well.

Now all I had to do was figure out how to get to BUD/S.

CHAPTER ELEVEN

I spent the first six months at HS-10 learning how to function as an air crew member and operate the systems in the back of assorted types of H-60 helicopters.

The H-60 is a broad class of U.S. military helicopter that includes the Sea Hawk, the Ocean Hawk, the Black Hawk, and a handful of others. At HS-10 they put us into several different kinds of simulators representing the various helicopter platforms we would soon be flying. One had a heavy sonar package; another, which we called a truck, was completely gutted and used mainly for combat and search-and-rescue exercises.

At the end of the six months, I got orders to HS-6. HS-6 was my first deployment. Yes, I was still in training—but I was now part of an actual, operational helicopter command. I was in the navy fleet now.

In the spring of 1995, HS-6 was deployed for six months to the western Pacific, on a WESTPAC. Our aircraft carrier was the USS *Abraham Lincoln*. We left port with an onboard population of about five thousand. The ship was like a small city unto itself.

We headed out west clear across the Pacific, stopping in Hawaii, Hong Kong, Thailand, and Australia. Our destination was the Persian Gulf. We spent the next four or five months there as the U.S. aircraft carrier presence. This was something like being a street cop. We weren't necessarily engaging anyone or seeing any action. We were there as a show of force, ready to be tapped whenever the need arose.

While this was an amazing experience, I was still focused on getting to BUD/S. I couldn't wait to earn as many qualifications as possible so I could finally get transferred there. My operational philosophy was: *I'm just going to do the best job I can and get all the quals, and then they'll let me go.*

And that included my tactical sensor operator (TSO) qual.

Over the course of my deployment on the USS *Lincoln*, I completed all the requirements needed to take the TSO test. The TSO ran the show and was the senior guy in the back of the aircraft. In essence, this would mean getting my qualification for crew chief.

Toward the end of the WESTPAC, I took my first check ride. I was ready to go and totally psyched.

"Check ride" means exactly that: from the moment we lifted off the flight deck and flew out over the gulf, they checked every move I made. They tested me on everything—language and terminology, correct procedures and sequences, how I operated every system I touched.

The entire check ride lasted about two hours. We touched down on the flight deck, and I turned to my instructors. "You did pretty well," they said, "but you need more experience." I stared at them, stunned. They were flunking me.

I knew I had passed the minimum requirements of the check ride. And I knew the instructors knew it too. But the instructors are given some latitude in the scoring process. There were a few senior guys in the squadron who were not exactly looking out for me. In the course of our deployment, I had knocked out all the requirements so fast that it kind of freaked a few of them out. They wanted to see me cut down to size.

I didn't argue, but now I had a negative mark on my record. Looking back, I realize that I shoulder some of the blame here: I had probably pushed too hard to take the test before being fully ready for it. Then again, if they'd already decided I wasn't ready, why did they even let me take the test in the first place?

CHAPTER TWELVE

A few days after I failed the TSO test, something happened that gave me one of the most vivid experiences in my life of great and terrible leadership, side by side.

We were on nighttime maneuvers over the Persian Gulf. Our pilot that night, Lieutenant Burkitt, was the sort of officer you can't help disliking. He was a slimy guy who annoyed officers and enlisted men alike. Lieutenant Burkitt's copilot, Kennedy, was a good guy and quite smart, though a little geeky. I served as crewman, along with Rich Fries, who was senior to me. In terms of rank and experience, I was the low man.

It had been a long night, and in order to make it all the way back to the *Lincoln*, we had to stop and refuel on a nearby destroyer. The night was pretty calm, but visibility was against us. There was absolutely no moon out. It was close to pitch black.

A destroyer's deck is pretty tight to land on, especially when compared to an aircraft carrier like the USS *Lincoln*. It was even more difficult on a night like this, with such low visibility. It was common operating procedure to slow the helo down to 90 knots (just over 100 mph), then open the cabin door and have one of the crewmen spot the deck and assist the pilot with verbal commands. On this occasion, the crewman doing the spotting was me.

As the helo slowed down to under 90 knots, I passed a message over the internal communications system that the door was coming open. The door cracked open, and I looked out to get a visual on the destroyer's lights. For some reason, I couldn't make anything out. I kept straining to see something and finally caught a glimpse of light—but it was at eye level, which I thought was strange. I looked down and realized that we were not where we were supposed to be. Our pilot had put us down at water level.

We were about to crash into the ocean.

"Altitude! Altitude!" I yelled. Rich immediately realized what was happening and joined in with me. I will never, in all my life, forget what happened next. Suddenly, we heard Lieutenant Burkitt's voice shrilly piercing through our yells. "What's happening?" he screamed. "I don't know what's happening! Oh God, oh God!"

He kept repeating that: Oh God, oh God.

For a split second Rich and I gaped at each other in disbelief. This was our pilot. This was our aircraft commander, screaming like a frightened schoolgirl.

We thought we were done for. I held tight to the cabin door. By now there was a foot of seawater in the main cabin, and any second we would be swamped and overrun with ocean: the point of no return. In my mind's eye, I could see the rotor blades sabering into the water and splintering into a thousand pieces, the helo flipping upside down and sinking into the gulf. Everything slowed way down and a stream of thoughts tore through my mind: *So this is why we go through the helo dunker training blindfolded. Is this really how it's going to end? No—I am not going to let this idiot Burkitt kill me!*

Then, in an instant, Kennedy, our copilot, somehow got himself together and hauled us up and out of the water. It was inches short of miraculous. Maybe it *was* miraculous.

The crew on the destroyer thought we had crashed and were goners for sure. They were shocked and thrilled to see us suddenly popping back up on radar.

Rich immediately replaced me on the door and rapidly talked Kennedy down onto the deck. Burkitt was an utter disaster the entire time, mumbling to himself.

A short investigation followed, but it went nowhere. The commanding officer (CO) of HS-6 didn't want his career to end over this incident. So he kept things tightly under wraps.

I don't know how he did it, but Kennedy saved all our lives that night. He deserved a medal for it. Instead, both he and Burkitt had their helicopter aircraft commander papers suspended.

I came away from that near-disaster with a resolve never to judge a person based on how they usually come across. Kennedy had always seemed like a smart and very competent guy, but not one I would have figured for a hero. You never know what people are capable of until you get to work with them, side by side.

I hope I get the chance to shake his hand again one day.

CHAPTER THIRTEEN

My strategy on how to get to BUD/S wound up back-firing on me. I had thought that if I gave everything my best, I would prove to my superiors that I was a hard worker and they would approve my assignment to BUD/S. In fact, the opposite happened. The better I did, the more valuable I became to my superiors. And the more reluctant they were to let me go.

When I say "they," I'm really talking about Chief Bruce Clarin. Clarin was an East Coast guy who hated being out on the West Coast. When he looked at me and some of my buddies, all he saw were guys he thought spent their whole lives surfing. To him, we were all slackers.

To this day, I am amazed that this guy made chief and was put in charge of an air crew shop. Nobody could stand him. Clarin was a walking, talking textbook illustration of how not to lead. He played favorites and rewarded people he liked, based not on any accomplish-ments, but purely on the fact that he just happened to like them. The guys he happened to like the most were also those who did the least amount of work and continually dragged the rest of us down.

About five months after returning from the WESTPAC, I submitted my first BUD/S application along with all necessary supporting documentation. It was quickly denied, all because of Clarin.

"You have all these quals," Clarin said. "Sorry, Webb, but I need you." Now I would have to stay with the squadron for at least another year and do a whole other six-month WESTPAC deployment.

This time we were stationed on the USS *Kitty Hawk*. This old boat was not a spanking new nuclear vessel like the USS *Lincoln*. It was a conventionally powered ship that had been around since the Vietnam War. Despite its age, that ship was clean. The crew was happy. Everything hummed along. This place was wired tight.

It didn't take long to understand why. That first night I heard the captain's voice come over the loudspeaker, welcoming us and giving us a brief rundown of what was happening the next day.

This had never happened on the *Lincoln*. The captain of that vessel hardly ever talked to his crew. The *Kitty Hawk* captain didn't address us only on that first day. He did it every one of the roughly 180 days we were aboard his ship.

"Good afternoon, shipmates, this is your captain," he would say. This is what we're doing, here's where we're going, these are the decisions we're making. He never revealed any details or specific plans that he shouldn't have, but he made sure that everyone felt included in what we were doing. As a result, morale was consistently high in a way it had not been on the *Lincoln*.

The two experiences were like night and day, and the difference came down to a single factor: Captain Steven John Tomaszeski and his leadership style. That crew loved their captain because he took care of them. I would have ridden that boat anywhere with Captain Tomaszeski, and I'm pretty sure every single person on board felt the same way.

I learned firsthand the importance of talking to your people, sharing the plan with them so they know where you're headed and the purpose behind it. It's not rocket science. Engage your crew. Have a dialogue. Let them know that you know they exist and that they're part of what you're doing. Leaving people in a vacuum is no way to lead, yet it's a mistake I've seen made way too many times.

I've tried to work this way every day. Whether I was running a covert op in Afghanistan or Iraq, reorganizing the SEAL sniper course in the States, or running a business after I left the service, I have tried and continue to try to keep everyone in the loop.

When I got back from that second WESTPAC in April 1997, there were orders waiting for me to report to BUD/S. It had been more than four years since I first set foot in Orlando for boot camp, and after a seemingly endless stream of obstacles I was finally on my way.

PART THREE

BECOMING A NAVY SEAL

CHAPTER FOURTEEN

Even though I already had my orders to go to BUD/S, I still had to demonstrate that I could pass the physical screening test (PST) before I could check into the program. Here is a quick overview of the minimum requirements applicants are required to *exceed*:

- a 500-yard (460-meter) swim, breaststroke or sidestroke, in 12.5 minutes or less (if you want to be seen as competitive, 9 minutes or less is better)
- at least 42 push-ups in 2 minutes (or at least 100 to be competitive)
- at least 50 sit-ups in 2 minutes (again, preferably 100 or more)
- at least 6 pull-ups from a dead hang (no time limit, but you want to shoot for a dozen or more)

- a 1.5-mile (2.4-kilometer) run in boots and pants, in under 11.5 minutes (better yet, under 9 minutes)

The day of the PST, all of us taking the test went down to the pool and did our swims. Then we hiked across the street, where we did our sequence of push-ups, sit-ups, and pull-ups. After that, we went outside for our 1.5-mile run, with boots.

We waited while they tallied up all our times. I could not believe it. My run time was twelve minutes—thirty seconds past the absolute maximum. Thirty seconds. Not only was I not competitive, I had actually failed. And I had failed badly. The memory of how I felt has stayed with me ever since. I had run smack into the last and toughest obstacle in my four-year quest to become a SEAL: myself.

It's easy to remember the times you excelled, the tests you passed, the things you've achieved. It's not as much fun to remember the times when you failed—or, even worse, failed miserably. Often, though, it's those failures, and not the wins, that end up leading you to a successful future.

I told myself that the important thing was not to feel sorry for myself. I practiced that test over and over until I knew beyond any shadow of a doubt that I had it nailed, and then I took it again. This time I passed, and it felt great. But I was still badly overestimating what kind of shape I was in.

I would find out soon enough.

On June 14, 1997, two days after my twenty-third birthday, I arrived in my dress whites on the main quarterdeck of the pretraining office in Coronado, California, to check in for BUD/S training. I had finally gotten in, but I knew that the odds of making it through the course were somewhere between one and three out of ten. Was I nervous? Oh, yeah.

I heard a roar like the crash of a gigantic surf coming from outside. The sound practically shook the building.

"Forty-nine! Fifty! Fifty-one!"

It was a BUD/S class doing their PT on the grinder, the legend-ary concrete-and-asphalt courtyard just outside the quarterdeck doors. I can still feel the shivers that ran up my spine as I heard the thunder those guys produced.

Outside, I saw about thirty hard-looking guys in brown shirts and tan Underwater Demolition Team (UDT) shorts doing PT in the courtyard with an instructor leading them through the exercises. The students were lined up on the black concrete, their feet posi-tioned atop staggered rows of small, white, frog-feet outlines painted onto the grinder's surface. Just off the edge of the concrete I saw the infamous brass bell. It was one of the most dreaded symbols of SEAL lore. If you reached the point where you decided you just couldn't take it, where the training was just too brutal to go on, you went and rang the bell three times. Then, you were gone. The brass bell was a one-way street out of BUD/S.

The bell had a well-worn braided rope trailing down from the ringer. More than a hundred green helmets lined the ground in a neat, mournful row. Each helmet was inscribed with the name and rank of one more would-be SEAL who never graduated.

"Sixty-one! Sixty-two! Sixty-three!"

It was good to finally see that thing, sitting there silently sus-pended in the air as if it were taunting me. Go on, sit there and wait, I almost murmured out loud. I'm never going to touch you.

CHAPTER FIFTEEN

My class, BUD/S Class 215, consisting of 220 men, started training the next week. There wouldn't be 220 of us for long.

BUD/S training is broken into three phases. Before the phases begin, there's a five-week indoctrination phase, called indoc. If you make it through that, you get to the phases. First Phase lasts six weeks and focuses on physical conditioning. It also includes Hell Week. Everyone in the navy knows about Hell Week. Hell Week is where you are pushed hard for five and a half days straight, with scarcely more than an hour's sleep per day, right up to the limits of physical and, especially, mental fortitude.

Second Phase consists of eight weeks of learning diving and water skills. Third Phase is nine weeks of land warfare. The whole thing adds up to more than seven months. The whole purpose boils down to this: to get you prepared for the *real* training, which comes *after* you graduate—or to spit you out.

• • •

During that first week of indoc we all did the initial BUD/S PT test over again, and not all of us passed. Just during indoc, we lost twenty guys. Boom. Ten percent of the class gone, and we hadn't even started First Phase yet.

Our first week in First Phase, this super-strong guy Lars, who I knew from the pre-BUD/S course I'd taken a year earlier, up and quit. Seeing a guy like that quit, especially so early on, was a revelation. I saw that this was not about who was the strongest or fastest. This was about sticking with it, and not giving up. Some guys might be able to knock out twice as many pull-ups as I could. That didn't necessarily mean, though, that they could handle the mental stress of constant, physically punishing workouts, during which you were yelled at and put down.

Over the coming months, I saw professional athletes, Olympic competitors, and some seriously tough and mean-looking dudes cry like babies as they walked across the grinder to go ring that brass bell. And I saw guys who weighed barely a hundred pounds take the most brutal physical and psychological punishment and keep on going.

I knew that the first six weeks were a weeding-out process— and that I was already a pretty good candidate for being one of the early weeds. As I had feared would happen, my long months on the USS *Kitty Hawk* had made me soft. Yes, we had been out on the ocean, but there was nowhere onboard that I could swim. And it is hard to run on a carrier, or find the place or time for serious workouts. So, before I checked into BUD/S I had taken a thirty-day leave to try to get back into some kind of condition. By the time I got to BUD/S, I thought I was in pretty decent shape. I learned that I was wrong on the first Monday morning of First Phase.

The men who become First Phase instructors are among the most physically fit people on the planet. They see themselves as guardians of the gate, and they are there to punish and bring the pain. They are the most feared, meanest, and ugliest guys you'll ever meet.

We had eight instructors for First Phase. Four of them would be a constant abrasive presence in our lives until we either made it to Second Phase or rang that bell.

One of them, Instructor Buchanan, gave us our initiation. Shirtless, cut like a jungle tiger, he stood on his four-foot podium looking down at us, ready to stomp us all, his vantage point ensuring that any weakness would be immediately identified and dealt with accordingly.

Then it started. First evolution, as they call it, was grinder PT, and he truly brought the pain: two hours of grueling punishment.

"Push-ups! Are you ready?" he shouted. "Hooyah!

"One! Two! Three! Four!"

After we passed one hundred I started to shake. I couldn't support my own body weight. My arms were on fire and giving out.

"On your feet . . . On your back . . . Push-ups! Ready? Begin! One! Two! . . . Flutter kicks, are you ready? One! Two! Three! . . . One hundred five! One hundred six . . . !"

I immediately stood out as a weak link. I kept falling behind. It wasn't just my physical condition. A lot of my classmates had come right from boot camp. Coming in as a fleet guy, I had a bit of seniority—and the instructors really don't like guys with a regular-navy mentality. It's culture clash. So, they give fleet guys a little bit of extra business.

Between my fleet background and my subpar physical shape, I stood out like a fly in a bowl of soup. With our last names neatly stenciled on our white shirts, they knew exactly who we all were, and all I kept hearing was our instructors shouting my name in conjunction with obscenities.

Soon I couldn't even tell what round I was supposed to be on. I remember hearing "Hit the surf zone!" multiple times. Hitting the surf zone involved running about five hundred yards out of the compound and down onto the beach, getting completely wet and sandy, and then sprinting back to the grinder for more punishment. The ice-cold Pacific Ocean was actually a welcome break—but soon

I was shivering uncontrollably and had sand in places I never thought possible.

Off to the side of the grinder there was a podium that held a roster book in which we signed up for remedial PT training sessions if we were so instructed. At the end of that first session, I was so instructed. I limped over to the podium and wrote my name in the book. Each morning I would now have to finish wolfing my breakfast earlier than everyone else and run back to start in on the remedial fitness training session and then join in on the regular training with everyone else.

Our day started at 5:00 A.M., on the beach, with grueling PT, and from there it was a never-ending endurance contest of both flesh and will. By the second week my hands were shredded. I developed two calluses on my left hand and three on my right, all five of them soon ripped off with a half-inch of flesh exposed from doing those wet and sandy push-ups on the beach. When the class corpsman applied a tincture of benzoin to seal the wounds and prevent infection, it felt like he was sticking a hot iron into each wound. I could barely stand up in the morning. My body was in complete breakdown.

It didn't matter: I was marked anyway. They have a saying in BUD/S training: "Don't be that guy." "That guy" is the one the instructors pick on, the one who's always on the receiving end of the worst punishment. Whatever you do, you do not want to be that guy.

I was that guy.

CHAPTER SIXTEEN

The following four weeks were utter misery. Everyone in the class quickly came to know me by name, because it was the name our instructors typically called out to do an extra hundred push-ups before dismissing the entire class for chow. It was humiliating, degrading, and painful. I would get up to forty-two! and suddenly hear, "Webb, start over!" While this was going on, the rest of the class was forced to remain in the lean and rest (that is, push-up) position and participate in my wretchedness. I can still hear the plaintive sounds of Class 215 pleading with me, "Webb, do a hundred good ones so we can get out of here!"

It was terrible to see those guys suffer because I was so out of shape. I quickly learned that as a team you are capable of great feats—but ultimately you are only as strong as your weakest link. Unfortunately, the weakest link here was me.

Our instructors kept adding new grueling routines that required us to swim or run farther, faster. We were now running a total of nineteen miles a day. A four-mile timed run had been added that we had to do on soft sand in thirty-two minutes or less, while wearing boots. I kept ending up in the back of the pack, a.k.a. the Goon Squad. Being in the Goon Squad meant that while everyone else was stretching, drinking water, and having a brief recoup, we few unfortunate dregs were getting destroyed doing bear crawls up and down the beach and push-ups in the surf. Day after day, I got Goon-Squaded every time. Soon I learned to push myself so hard that I threw up as I ran. Eventually I began just making the cutoff to stay out of the Goon Squad.

Then, of course, there was the dreaded O-course, in fifteen minutes or less. The BUD/S O-course was built for pain and suffering. It is one of the best-constructed obstacle courses in the world. In start-to-finish order, it consists of:

- Parallel bars. You shimmy along a set of steel tubes canted at an upward angle for twelve feet.
- Tires. Multiple tires that you have to step through rapidly.
- Low wall. An eight-foot plywood wall you jump up and swing over.
- High wall. This one is about double the height of the low wall; you use a thick rope to climb up and over.
- Low barbed-wire crawl. Exactly what it sounds like: stay low or hook skin.
- Hundred-foot-high cargo net. Climb up and over.
- Balance logs. You run along a series of rolling logs while keeping your balance (or trying to).
- Hooyah logs. ("Hooyah" is the ultimate SEAL catchall word, meaning everything from "Yes, Instructor!" to any obscenity you can think of.) This is a pile of three-foot logs that you step up and over while holding your hands up over your head.
- Rope transfer. Climb up one rope, transfer to another, then slide down.

- Dirty Name. Aptly named. A double set of log beams: You jump up, grab the first log beam, and pull yourself up, then get to your feet and jump up and onto the higher log beam, swing around and over, and drop down to the sand. This station is a rib-breaker, which is how it got its name.
- Weaver. Metal bars spaced about three feet apart and shaped like a shallow triangle. Weave over and under, all the way up, then down, and you're out.
- Burma Bridge. Climb a fifteen-foot rope, then transition to an unstable rope bridge, cross the bridge, and slide down a second fifteen-foot rope on the other side.
- Hooyah logs again.
- Slide for Life. A four-story set of platforms with an angled rope that slopes down about a hundred feet to the bottom. Climb to the top, then mount the rope from the bottom with your legs wrapped around, hang with your arms, and worm your way down. Next, transition to an assault style on top position (much quicker). Disrespect this one and you have broken bones, which happened to guys constantly. Fall off and you have a good chance of getting medically disqualified from BUD/S.
- Rope swing. Grab the rope on the run and swing up, then let go at just the right moment to hop up and onto a high balance log beam.
- Tires again.
- Incline wall. Scoot up, slide over and down.
- Spider wall. A high plywood-and-log wall you climb up and shimmy along sideways. Similar to rock climbing, it's all about finger and toe strength.
- Vaults. A series of logs set at intervals. Jump up and over each one on your way to a sprint finish.

For the first few obstacles, I had no problem. The Weaver slowed me down, and by the time I got to the top of the Slide for Life I was whipped. Soon I found myself hanging on for dear life by my legs, four stories up and upside down. All my grip strength was gone, and my hands were burning from the torn calluses. In a last-ditch effort not to fall, I hooked both elbows over the top of the rope and attempted to recover some grip strength.

Instructor Kowalski screamed at me. "Webb, you have two seconds to let go of that rope with your elbows, and you already used them up!" He ordered me to let go and shimmy down.

I unhooked my elbows and continued to hang upside down by my legs, delaying the inevitable four-story fall. A memory flashed through my mind of a hapkido class I'd taken when I was a kid, when we'd been taught the importance of knowing how to survive a fall. That memory, together with some dumb luck, saved me from getting too badly hurt. I let go, and a terrifying moment later I hit the ground like a sack of ready-mix concrete.

Instructor Kowalski walked over, kicked me in the stomach, and said, "Hey, you all right?"

"Hooyah, Instructor Kowalski," I managed to get out.

"Well, then, get up and get going!" he yelled.

I got up and got going.

CHAPTER SEVENTEEN

In the water skills training in First Phase they walked us through the basic skills of underwater demolition: breath hold (no tanks), long underwater swims, underwater knot tying, and the like. The point was to get used to the water, push our limits, and realize that we could go a lot farther than we thought we could.

I'd done drown-proofing in Search and Rescue school. Here it was again, but taken up several notches. My hands were tied behind my back and my feet were tied together. Then I was tossed into a twenty-foot dive tank, where I had to survive for an hour doing various exercises like diving down and picking up objects on the bottom of the pool with my mouth.

We did an underwater breath-hold fifty-meter (164 feet) swim, which went like this: jump into the pool feet first (no pushing off the wall), do a somersault, then go fifty meters down and back, holding your breath the whole way. Guys popped up to the surface like goldfish corpses. Not that they had quit intentionally—they had just passed out.

Another water test was the underwater knot-tying trial. You submerge, tie your first knot, then wait for your instructor to inspect and approve it. Once your work is okayed, you go up to surface for a moment, catch a breath, then go down to tie the next knot, and on through a series of five knots in all.

Typically the instructor takes his time inspecting your knot, looking it over very slowly. Not because he needs to, but because what he's really doing is trying his best to force you to run out of air.

I don't know why, but Instructor Shoulin really had it in for me. So it should have come as no surprise when he singled me out during the underwater knot-tie exercise.

Instructor Shoulin didn't know that I practically grew up under water. I may have been at the bottom of the heap in basic PT, but when it came to water skills, I felt I could do anything they threw at me.

We dove down under, Instructor Shoulin on my tail like a shark tracking a baby seal. I tied my first knot. He looked it over, real slow. He couldn't find anything wrong with it, but he took forever.

Finally he looked over and gave me the thumbs-up: *This one's okay, you can surface now.* Only I didn't surface. Instead, I moved on and started tying my second knot. I finished the second knot and he inspected and approved it, more quickly this time. I ignored his you-can-surface-now gesture once again. I started in on my third knot.

That was it. Instructor Shoulin couldn't hold out any longer— he went up to the surface to gasp for air. He was really steamed. I had embarrassed him. I was pretty sure I'd wind up paying for it, too.

CHAPTER EIGHTEEN

By the fifth week of First Phase, I was a wreck: exhausted, humiliated, just about beaten into a corner. Then one afternoon, just a few days before Hell Week, it all came to a head.

Every afternoon we formed seven-man boat crews, grabbed our heavy rubber boats, threw them up on top of our heads, and ran to the beach to get tortured for a while. On this particular afternoon we were on our way out to the beach when Instructor Shoulin called me over. The other three toughest First Phase instructors were with him.

Uh-oh.

We headed to a section of beach where it was just us.

"Drop, Webb," said one of them. And the physical punishment began. They had me do push-ups, flutter kicks, the whole works. The whole time all four of them shoveled sand in my face and yelled at me, at the top of their lungs.

"You are worthless, Webb! You're weighing your

whole class down. You are a one-man walking disaster. You don't belong here. Do you even know how much everyone wants you gone? You need to quit."

On and on for the next hour. It was beyond brutal. I could feel how intensely they wanted me to get up, limp away, and ring that brass bell.

The worst of it was, I knew they were right. There was a reason they were singling me out. I was physically out of shape, and that had been affecting the entire class. That bothered me. It bothered me so much it is something I've stayed aware of and careful about to this day. If you show up late, if you don't have your gear together, or your facts together, or whatever it is you need to have together, then you affect your whole team.

However, if I was not physically where I needed to be, I was very tough mentally. And what SEAL training really tests is your mental strength. It is designed to push you mentally to the brink, over and over again, until you are hardened and able to take on any task with confidence, regardless of the odds—or until you break.

I was not about to break.

People have asked me if I ever thought about quitting SEAL training. The answer is never—not once. Lying there facedown in the sand with these four hardcase instructors doing their level best to break me, something else happened instead: I got what we call a fire in the gut.

Of the four, it was Instructor Buchanan who was the most in my face that day. So I looked up at him, nailed him with the coldest stare I could muster, and said, "Instructor Buchanan, the only way you're getting me out of here is in a body bag."

He glared back at me, gauging me, weighing my intent. I meant every word, and he knew it. He took one step back and jerked his head, gesturing up the beach. "Get back to your crew," he said.

From that point on, my experience in BUD/S completely turned the corner. Those instructors left me alone. When Hell Week started, it was almost anticlimatic. *Welcome to my world*, I felt like saying to the other guys. I'd been playing these games throughout First Phase.

There is another saying in BUD/S: Ideally you want to become the gray man. In other words, you become invisible, nobody notices you, because you do everything so perfectly you never stand out.

I had gone from "that guy" to gray man.

CHAPTER NINETEEN

Hell Week was as brutal as all the legends say, and then some. From the morning it began, my classmates started winking out like cheap lightbulbs.

The first night, they disoriented us. We were up all night, and that was only the beginning, because we were going to be up for five days and nights straight. If you were hanging in there by the third night you didn't have a lot of company, because most of the guys had already quit.

"Steel pier" was the name of one of the things they had us do. At two in the morning, they walked us into the ocean and threw us on a steel barge, where we lay half naked, our body temperature dropping to hypothermia levels. Then, just as I didn't think we could hang on to consciousness any longer, they had us get up, jump in the water—and then climb out and get back on the pier. For four hours. We heard the doleful sound of the brass bell ringing in the dark, again and again.

As hard as it was, the physical punishment wasn't

the worst of it. It was the psychological torture that broke so many of us and kept that brass bell ringing. We never knew what they were going to pitch at us next. Those five days were designed to throw us off balance, and it worked.

On day three they put us in a tent to get some sleep. We laid our weary bones down on thin, uncomfortable cots that to us felt like heaven. We drifted off—until about fifty minutes later, when we heard a voice shouting.

"Time to go hit the surf!"

I'll tell you what it's like when you have just gone through three solid days of physical punishment, around the clock, and then you finally have the chance to get to sleep, only to be yanked out of it again less than an hour later: it's torture. And that is no figure of speech. This is actually one of the most common techniques used to torture prisoners of war.

I opened my eyes. Guys around me were completely disoriented, jerking upright and staring around desperately, literally not knowing where they were or what was going on. Next thing we knew we were all running out to go lie on the freezing cold beach, right down in the surf, faces toward the ocean so the waves could wash sand and saltwater into our eyes and noses and mouths.

Even worse than this, though, were the chow runs. We carried those big rubber boats on our heads everywhere, even to chow.

When it was time to eat, they raced us, with our boats, to the mess hall, where they had us run around a small building. They let a few crews at a time in to eat. When it was our crew's turn to eat, we quickly put our boat down, ran inside, shoveled down the food, then ran out again.

Sometimes when we got back outside, we were a few people short. Those guys never showed up again. They were out. The instructors reshuffled the crews, and off we went again.

One night we did an exercise called Round the World. Each boat crew paddled its boat out some twenty miles to a checkpoint and then back. It took about eight hours and was all done, of course, at night.

The last day they put us on the beach in a fenced-off area they had filled with seawater. They called this seawater swamp the Demo Pit, but it was nothing more than a muddy bog strung with rope bridges. We stood there, exhausted, caked head to toe with mud, barely able to stay on our feet—and they started firing grenade simulators at us.

At this point we were zombies. I don't know how fast I moved, or even if I moved at all. I know some guys just dropped into the bog and lay there.

Then they ran us up to the compound and lined us up on the grinder. Someone said, "Class 215, secured from Hell Week."

Secured. We were done?!

It was unreal. We had been suffering so badly it felt like time had slowed down and stretched out until the punishment was a raw experience of eternity. Suddenly it was over and we were being handed our brown T-shirts.

Secured.

CHAPTER TWENTY

When the seven weeks of Second Phase started our class was down to 70 of the original 220.

BUD/S is fundamentally a course in underwater demolition, so the focus is on water skills. And the dive phase is, in a way, the core of the whole course. Because I was already a strong diver, I thought this phase would be a breeze.

Dive phase was no joke. Yes, they were now focusing more on teaching us specific skills than on raking us over the coals to sift out the early quitters. Now that we were wearing brown T-shirts, they treated us with a little more respect. It was still brutal.

Our new instructors were just as intent as our First Phase instructors on letting us know they were not messing around. Right away, they had us on the ground doing push-ups, yelling and screaming in our faces. Whatever else we were doing—our classroom work, dive training, instruction in scuba, how to use a rebreather, and other key dive skills—the basic physical training kept going in the background, every single day. It got harder and harder, the bar was raised higher and higher, and the times got shorter and shorter. Our conditioning runs went from four miles to six miles to eight miles. All our minimum times started dropping. The O-course time dropped from fifteen to eleven minutes.

While we were in the classroom most of the day, it was not what you would think of as a normal classroom. For example, they kept buckets of ice water (which we had to keep filling) placed above us on racks over our heads. If someone started nodding off in class, the instructor could tug on a string and ice water would pour down over the entire table. This was not community college. This was BUD/S.

About halfway through the dive phase we had a test called Pool Comp (short for "pool competence"). Pool Comp is Second Phase's version of Hell Week.

I jumped into the combat training tank with my gear, a set of double aluminum 80s and an aqualung rig, and sank down about fifteen or twenty feet. Suddenly three instructors were on top of me—they call this a surf hit. Without warning they ripped my mask from my face and yanked off my fins, leaving me with nothing but a set of tanks and a regulator in my mouth.

Then they started in on me, one of them ripping the regulator hose out of my mouth and quickly tying it in knots.

I hadn't known exactly what to expect, but I knew it would be something like this, and I was as ready for it as I could be. That's the drill in Pool Comp. They put you through five or six really bad situations underwater, and you have to get out of them. If you come up to the surface, you fail.

I also knew that right at the end of the ordeal we would be hit with a truly messed-up situation, something so difficult that it's essentially impossible to get out of. This is called the whammy. You deal with it as best you can, then signal that you're okay and head up to the surface. You're not expected to get out of the whammy, just to stick it out as long as you can.

I reached the point where I was sucking air directly out of the tank valve, because I absolutely could not undo the knot that guy had put in my hose. I'd been down there for maybe fifteen minutes, getting worked over by several instructors, and it had seemed like an eternity. Now I was sucking in whatever air I could get out of that tank, trying to breathe in the little air bubbles that were leaking off my regulator. Finally I figured there was no way out of this whammy, so I signaled and headed up.

As I broke the surface, my instructor said, "Webb, that wasn't the whammy."

"What?" I gasped. That had to be the whammy. There was no way anyone could get that hose untied. I could have stayed down longer, but I was positive my test was over. Well, it wasn't.

I practically felt nauseous. I had failed Pool Comp—and we only got two tries.

It was three days before I could retest. Then I went back down in the tank, and no matter what they threw at me, I stayed down there. I don't even remember what the whammy was like, because I was so focused on staying down, no matter what.

Finally an instructor swam down and started shaking me, yanking me up by the hair and making urgent *Come up!* gestures. My whammy was over.

I was relieved I passed, but it still blew my mind that it had taken two tries. I was supposed to excel in anything water related. This was another lesson I would strive to remember always and in all situations: don't make assumptions going into a challenge—ever. No matter what you know, or think you know, put your ego in check and see what you can learn.

CHAPTER TWENTY-ONE

We moved onto Third Phase down another twenty guys. Third Phase is nine weeks of SEAL-style land warfare, basic soldiering skills. It includes explosives and demolition, marksmanship, land navigation, and reconnaissance.

Things didn't get any easier. Our O-course time dropped from eleven minutes to ten and a half. The four-mile timed run went from twenty-nine minutes to twenty-eight, and they added a thirteen-mile run, in boots.

Now, we got camouflage outfits and web gear, which we call second-line gear. (First-line gear would be the clothes you're wearing, your pants, your belt, and so forth. Second-line or web gear, also called H-gear, is your chest harness, which carries all your magazines for your bullets, your compass, and your other kit. Third-line gear is your backpack.)

We started out doing basic firearms training, both

rifle and pistol, first with classroom study and then on to practical application in labs, taking apart the weapons and putting them back together. We also did some shooting.

The bulk of this part of Third Phase is a big land navigation course up in the Laguna Mountains east of San Diego. We packed up our gear and a load of MREs (Meals, Ready-to-Eat) and headed up there.

After a few days of orientation, we spent a week of classes doing map and compass work. The whole thing culminated in an individual land nav test, almost like a race. We all knew that if we didn't pass, we didn't graduate.

For the test the instructors had planted a series of navigation points out among the mountains. At each point there was an ammo box with a unique code inside, and when we reached that point we would open the box, then radio in that number along with our coordinates. This way they'd know we were on the right mountain. Then we had to move on to the next point. We each had to hit all the points and hit them in the right sequence.

I ran into one of the guys out there. He stared at me, frantic. "I think I just missed my last point!" he blurted, then pointed off into the distance. "I'm supposed to be on that mountain way over there!" He went trundling off frantically through the forest. Poor guy.

I was lucky. I did not have much difficulty with the navigation. Here again, I think my background helped. Growing up on the sailboat, being around charts and maps and compasses, I'd learned how to find my way around without street signs, storefronts, and all the usual landmarks most of us learn as kids. As a result, I finished my test a few hours early.

Even so, I would have rather done Hell Week twice than have gone through Third Phase. They just kept cranking up the pressure, pushing us to our limits, adding on layers of physical and mental stress, sleep deprivation, and increased responsibility (like working with demolition and live fire while exhausted). It never let up for a moment.

The day after the land nav test we packed up our site, loaded the trucks, and were headed back to civilization. It seemed like we had all made it through. But I found out that for me, at least, it wasn't over yet.

On the way back from the test site, my left quad suddenly seized up, just above the knee. It was excruciating—and crippling. I don't know if it was all the adrenaline coursing through my system from the land nav, or the sheer cold, or what caused it, but when I woke up the next morning I could barely put any weight on my left leg.

I was now in deep trouble. Third Phase wasn't over yet. To meet the criteria for Third Phase we needed to pass at least two out of four timed runs. I still needed one more run—and I could barely walk.

I went into BUD/S Medical and told the guy I had a bad quad. It was my first time there in six months of physically grueling training.

The guy took care of me, got me on crutches—and I lucked out. It happened that we were just then hitting Christmas break. For the next two weeks all we had to do was show up for one PT a day, and those didn't count toward our passing. That gave me two weeks to heal.

When January came, there was no more putting it off. I had to get out there and finish that four-mile run, and do it in less than thirty minutes. Strange to say, the instructors were quite encouraging. They knew I was dealing with an honest injury and wasn't sandbagging it. They could see I was in pain.

Four miles is about 6,436 meters, and a meter is about my stride, which means that during that run, my left leg came down hard 3,218 times, and each time was agony. It took everything I had, but I finished in time.

CHAPTER TWENTY-TWO

After Christmas we shipped out to San Clemente Island, about eighty miles off the coast of San Diego. This island is completely dedicated to navy activities, and the SEALs have the northwest end to themselves with a BUD/S camp out there we call the Rock.

Once we all got out there, our instructors said, "Hey, fellas, no one can hear you scream out here. You're pretty far away from the flagpole," meaning base command on the coast. There was not a lot of oversight here, no commanding officers strolling by at lunch to see how things were going. These instructors had us to themselves, and they made sure we knew it. These were our final four weeks before graduating—or not graduating. They would make sure we each earned it.

There was some sort of physical exercise before each meal, and how well we did determined what our meal experience was going to be. Every meal, we had to earn the right to eat dry. That's right. Dry.

For breakfast we all lined up outside the compound,

separated out by squad. On their signal, they told us, one squad would sprint over to Frog Hill, a big hill nearby, and climb to the top as fast as possible. The first four to reach the top would come down and go eat breakfast. The three stragglers (there were seven men to a squad) would come down off the hill, go jump into the freezing cold ocean, and then take breakfast outside, covered with sand and soaking wet.

On the signal we lit out at a dead sprint—seven guys clawing their way up this hill. My lungs were burning. I am not a great runner, and I could still feel that pulled quad. Every morning I found myself smack in the middle of the pack, worried I would fall behind the cutoff point and end up with sand up my ass while I wolfed cold eggs. Somehow I managed to make it into the top four every day.

That was breakfast. For lunch, we had to bang out a minimum of a hundred push-ups with all our gear on. If we didn't get all our push-ups in on time, we ate lunch wet.

For dinner we had to do an eighty-foot rope climb and then a minimum of twenty pull-ups with full kit. Do it, or get wet.

Every morning I woke up with the same thought: I hope I don't have to eat wet today.

By this point there were about forty of us. Of those 40, 17 had been medically rolled in from a previous BUD/S class. They had been pulled from their first class for medical reasons. By the time they were healed and ready to go back to BUD/S, our class was under way, so they joined us. All this meant that of the 220 who had started our class six months earlier, only 23 of us were left.

As part of our final training exercise, we went through a major nighttime op on a Zodiac, a large inflatable boat. The surf was big that night, and at one point we abruptly got a signal to come in. Our lane grader, the SEAL instructor who was evaluating our whole operation, was worried because the water was getting rough. I knew this particular section of beach: we were dangerously close to a seriously rocky shoreline. Beaching a rubber boat on a shoreline filled with sharp rocks is not something you want to take lightly. It can kill you.

Our boat crew leader told us to start heading back in. I tried to get him to wait so we could time it around the waves so we wouldn't get wrecked coming into the shore. But he wouldn't listen. So there was nothing I could do about it. We were going right then, immediately. Oh, man, I thought, this is not going to be good.

We started paddling like crazy, but I knew there was no way we would make it in time. I could feel the swell coming. Sure enough, we started rising, then lowering, and then the next rise was bigger—and then I knew we were about to get hit.

A moment later a monster wave broke right on top of us. The next thing I knew I was the only one left in the boat, and I was hurtling toward shore. If I didn't want to get sliced to ribbons on that treacherous shoreline, I was going to have to manage the entire Zodiac myself. This was bad. In fact, there was no way this situation could get any worse.

Darting a look backward, I caught a glimpse of something at the stern of the Zodiac. I looked closer—it was someone's fingers. One of the guys had managed to hold on. Then a head bobbed into view. It was Mike.

Here I was, alone in our runaway Zodiac with everyone else back there somewhere in the ocean, with Mike hanging on to the stern for dear life—and we were about to hit the rocks.

I had one thing going for me. I still had seconds' worth of the lull that follows after a big set of waves breaks—but only seconds. Somehow I got control of the Zodiac and managed to surf the thing safely up over the rocks and close enough in that I could touch bottom. I glanced back for a split second. No more fingers on the stern.

I jumped out and scrabbled for a foothold in the rocks, then grabbed the Zodiac and started hauling it in. As I approached the shoreline I hopped back into the boat to make sure everything was strapped down—and felt something strange at my feet. There was something *underneath* the boat, something pushing up.

No, not something. Someone.

I threw myself out of the Zodiac, grabbed it with both hands, and heaved with all my might to free it from the pull of the water. Then I managed to flip it over. A figure came gasping up out of the surf like a creature in a horror movie.

It was Mike! He'd been trapped under the Zodiac for more than two minutes. We stood there on the shore, Mike leaning on me while he caught his breath. One of the instructors came running up to us. I figured he was coming to see how Mike was. Instead the instructor demanded to know if all the weapons had made it back. And that instructor was Instructor Shoulin.

He was helping out in Third Phase—but it felt like the guy had been put on this Earth to find me and torture me.

Fortunately for all of us, we'd had our guns clipped in tight on the Zodiac. These were real weapons, and if any of us had lost one we would have been in serious trouble. Losing a gun is a career-ender for a full-fledged SEAL, let alone a BUD/S student. If we had lost any of those weapons, most likely we would all have been kicked out. It would have been a big problem for our instructors, too.

We didn't lose any firearms, and we didn't lose any people, either. Within another half minute everyone else was coming in to shore. Our crew leader came up to me and said, "Man, we should have waited for that set." I didn't reply.

CHAPTER TWENTY-THREE

We had made it. Two hundred twenty men had started BUD/S. Just over twenty of us had completed it. We still had many more months of training to go before we would become SEALs, but when I stepped off the plane back in San Diego I felt like I could conquer anything. Nothing I've ever experienced quite compares with how it felt to know that I had made it all the way through BUD/S.

The night before graduation, it's tradition for all the graduating students to take the instructors out.

At some point I turned around and was face-to-face with Instructor Shoulin.

It was the weirdest thing. Here was this maniac who had done everything in his power to get me to quit, this guy that I hated—and we were at a guys' night out together.

"You know, Webb, I hated you," he said. *Hey, don't hold back*, I thought but didn't say. *Tell me what you really think.* He continued talking in his soft, icy killer's voice, looking straight ahead, speaking almost as if I weren't there.

"I did not want you to make it through," he said. "I thought we could make you quit."

He stopped talking again. Maybe he expected me to say something. Maybe not. In any case, I kept my mouth shut and waited to see if he had anything else to say. He did.

"But you shoved it in our faces. You stepped up. I watched you turn a corner—and I was impressed." Then he quietly added, "You earned our respect."

Those few minutes were worth everything I'd been through.

CHAPTER TWENTY-FOUR

After BUD/S, while my training to become a SEAL continued, it was time to be assigned to a specific SEAL team. I had to list my top three picks in order of priority. I wanted to be wherever the action was. It was 1998. There wasn't much conflict happening in the world, or at least no major clashes in which our forces were directly involved. I figured, though, if anything important was going to happen it would be in the Middle East. So my top pick was Team Three, which had the Middle East as its area of operations (AO). What's more, Team Three had a really good reputation. I then listed Team Five and Team One in that order. I was elated when the assignments came down: I had gotten Team Three.

I learned very quickly that new guys are better seen and not heard. We hadn't yet earned our SEAL Tridents, and we were still on a six-month probation period. The guys on the team never let us forget that we weren't officially SEALs yet. So I did exactly the same thing I'd done back as a new guy in HS-6. I put my head down, kept my mouth shut, and made sure I did a good job at everything they threw at me.

The next big step was to class up to SEAL Tactical Training (STT), a three-month intensive program of advanced training. STT was where we would really start getting into close-quarters battle tactics; going room to room; shooting thousands of rounds on the range; and more challenging land navigations and extended dives.

This brought me face-to-face with a major challenge. I needed to demonstrate that I could perform up to par when it came to shooting a weapon.

There had been a bit of shooting in boot camp. We'd had a little time on the range as part of SAR training and again as part of BUD/S, but not much. When it came to firearms, I was green as the grass.

Right off the bat we spent a week at the Naval Training Center (NTC) range, where we shot a variety of firearms, including the M4 semiautomatic assault rifle, SIG SAUER P226 semiautomatic 9mm pistol, the Heckler & Koch USP .45 semiautomatic pistol (USP stands for "universal self-loading pistol"), and the H&K MP5 9mm submachine gun. The designation "submachine" means it fires subsonic rounds. A subsonic bullet travels slower than the speed of sound and doesn't make the snap! you hear when a bullet travels faster than the speed of sound.

This was all new to me, and I found myself seriously behind the curve. Almost from day one I had instructors all over me, wanting to know what my problem was. It was like being back at the beginning of BUD/S. Suddenly I was that guy again. I had to get it together.

After a week at the NTC we went out to the La Posta Mountain training facility, about an hour's drive east of San Diego. A few weeks in, they started running us through combat drills they call stress courses. Stress course is right. For me, this was the moment of truth. I would either step up my game or show up as lame.

It wasn't that I was worried about flunking out. This was about reputation. As I was coming to learn, reputation is like a house that, once you burn it down, is almost impossible to build again. This is true in business, in communities, in the world at large—but in the SEAL community it's true times ten. Nothing is worth as much as your reputation.

The drills took place on a course that was set up with barricades every ten to twenty feet. The idea was to spring through the course, take cover at each barricade and shoot different kinds of targets, hitting as many as you could within a given time. Run fast, stay hidden, shoot the bad guys.

When my turn came, I checked my M4 assault rifle, cleared my head, and breathed steadily. I knew the next few minutes would stay with me in the team's eyes, for better or for worse, for months to come.

The instructor yelled "Go!" I tore off on a twenty-foot sprint to take cover behind the first barricade. I peered around the right edge, down low, and engaged the target. Crack! Ping! These were steel knockdown targets. You hit one and it flips down backward. Crack! Ping! Crack! Ping!

After firing off a few quick rounds, I sprinted to the next barricade, where I repeated the process, and then to the next. At the third station there were half a dozen head poppers, targets that suddenly popped up with just their heads showing. The goal was to take out all six in rapid succession. I fired off six rounds, and then took off for the next station.

A few stations later, with plenty of targets still left to shoot, I ran out of ammo. They had designed it this way on purpose. They wanted to see how we did when our primary weapon went dry. I swept my rifle to the side, letting it swing on its sling by its own weight, immediately drew my pistol and fired off several more rounds at the remaining targets, then holstered the sidearm, grabbed my rifle, and brought it back up as I sprinted to take cover and reload. Cover, not concealment. We'd been drilled on the difference. Cover is when you hide behind something that can actually provide you with physical protection. Concealment means you're hiding behind something that shields you visually, like a bush, but the other guy can shoot through the bush and hit you. I took cover, dropped my depleted M4 mag, slammed in a fresh magazine, loaded a fresh mag in my pistol, too, in case I needed it, then sprinted off to engage the next series of targets.

The whole thing was a whirlwind—just one unbroken stream of actions and reactions. It was over before I even had time to think.

Our instructor did a double take that was almost comical. I looked around and realized the other guys were all staring at me. I hadn't missed a single shot. I had smoked the whole course.

I'd redeemed myself.

CHAPTER TWENTY-FIVE

We spent the next six weeks doing our desert warfare phase, in the desert around a place called Niland. It was summer and the temperature hit 115°F most days. It sometimes got so hot we couldn't put blasting caps in the ground for our demolition exercises, because the heat of the ground would set them off.

They put us through our paces in land nav and land warfare exercises, simulated drills where we'd come up against enemy contact and have to fight our way out of it. We also did some advanced demolition work there as part of an assault package. We'd go into a mock village, stage a prisoner snatch, shoot up the place, then set our C-4 charges and pull smoke on them. We'd have fifteen minutes to get out before it all blew.

At Niland we were introduced to some of the heavier machine guns, the .50-caliber and .60-caliber, and we also got some practice on the Carl Gustav, an 84mm recoilless rifle handheld rocket launcher, and got to fire some LAW (light antitank weapon) rockets.

Although we mostly used live fire, for some exercises we used a laser setup called Multiple Integrated Laser Engagement System (MILES), which fires blanks, a little like playing paintball. We used this system when we went up against each other in teams in OppFor (Oppositional Force) exercises.

The focus, though, was not on that kind of force-on-force situation. Going in en masse and taking down a known force, like charging a machine-gun nest, is not a typical SEAL mission. We're not the marines. Our preferred methodology is to insert ourselves in the middle of the night when no one's looking, hit them, and get out. We're not really there to fight; we're there to tip the scales. At Niland, our focus was on demolition—and on getting a taste of what it takes to survive in the most inhumanly hot conditions imaginable.

Near the end of our time at Niland, they took us out in the desert for a six-hour land nav course. It was miserable out, August in the desert. A few hours after that they took us on a twelve-mile timed run with weapons and full rucksack loaded with fifty pounds of gear. We started in after dinner, about eight in the evening. In Niland in August, eight o'clock is still hot. And the time we had to beat just added to the challenge.

Out of a class of some eighty guys only six of us finished. The rest couldn't continue or quit because of dehydration and other complications from the extreme heat.

It felt really good to finish that run. But the feeling didn't last long. An instructor walked up to me and said, "Hey, why is your weapon dirty?"

I looked at my weapon. Some dirt had gotten on it, probably when I had fallen over with severe leg cramps at the water station. It's a code they had pounded into us: you take care of the team's gear first, then you help your buddy, and once all that's done, then you take care of yourself. You always make sure all your team is squared away before you go hop in the shower. It's a code I believe in. It's a great value to have. But just then I really didn't want to hear it. I guess the look on my face said all that because the instructor nodded and walked away.

CHAPTER TWENTY-SIX

Our time at Niland was followed up with a few weeks at Camp Pendleton in a block of extensive land nav training, followed by four weeks of combat swimmer training off the coast of San Diego. I graduated from SEAL Tactical Training on August 14, 1998, and headed back to the team to get back to work—and to prepare for my Trident board.

The SEAL Trident is the only badge in the navy that has no rank. When you wear that Trident, anywhere you go in the military, people get out of your way, no matter what rank they are, because they know what it means to earn that thing.

The day finally came, a Wednesday in late 1998, six of us standing in the hallway in our starched, pressed desert cammies (the standard uniform, made of camouflage material). We waited together out in the hall on the top floor of the Team Three area. One by one, they called us in. Each guy was in there probably no more than thirty minutes, but it seemed like hours. When my turn came, I went in and sat down in the center of a horseshoe of instructors, who immediately started in on me, firing away with their questions. The questions were about weapons specs, communications, first aid, diving, flying, and more.

I had to have the answers all down pat, and I had to answer fast. It was incredibly intimidating.

But I passed.

At that Friday's assembly an instructor pinned a Trident to my uniform. I was no longer a search-and-rescue swimmer, a navy regular, a BUD/S student, a Team Three member on probation, an STT student.

I was a Navy SEAL.

The next instant, a throng of guys started running toward me—and I took off as fast as I could. There is a SEAL tradition: once you have your Trident, you get thrown in the ocean, fully clothed. I did my best to outrun them and throw myself in, but no dice. They grabbed me and tossed me in the Pacific. Then they hauled me out again, soaking wet, took me back onshore, and started pounding my Trident.

This is another navy tradition. A normal pin has a little metal or plastic backing that secures it on, like a tie tack, and keeps the pin from sticking into your skin, but there was no backing on my Trident.

They pounded in my Trident, right over my heart. It felt good. It was and remains one of the proudest moments of my life.

PART FOUR

ONE OF AMERICA'S DEADLIEST SNIPERS

CHAPTER TWENTY-SEVEN

A few days before receiving my Trident, I found out that I was being placed into GOLF platoon, one of the A-list platoons. I would spend the next two years with these guys.

GOLF platoon was an odd assortment of characters, a strange but solid mix of personalities. Having the skills and the objective qualifications is one thing, but there's something you can't quite measure in tests that has to be there too. Chemistry. And for us, the chemistry was great. With SEALs in general, you're dealing with a group of people who are pretty extreme, every single one an alpha male. Each guy is constantly keeping the others in check, but while they may beat each other up, when it comes down to it, it's all for one.

Around this time I also met Gabriele, the woman I would go on to marry and have three incredible kids with.

The training continued. We spent the next eighteen months in a lengthy workup, a seemingly endless procession of training blocks that took me all over the country and through some of the finest programs in the world. We would spend three or four weeks with the platoon, stationed in Coronado, then go off to a specialized school somewhere in the country for a training block, then rotate back home and repeat the cycle.

The truth is, SEALs never stop training. When we aren't actually deployed we're always learning new skills, continuing to hone our existing skills, and keeping ourselves in peak physical condition.

In the spring of 2000 our eighteen-month workup concluded with an operational readiness exam (ORE), conducted off San Clemente Island. There were some tricky issues with water currents on the way back in, and things got sketchy. By the time we got back to rendezvous with our vessel, I had run out of air and had a headache, but we passed the exercise. GOLF platoon was certified and operationally ready to rotate overseas to serve in an alert status, which the platoon would do after a little downtime.

Before this could happen, though, something else happened, unexpectedly, that changed the course of my navy career.

One day shortly after our ORE, my buddy Glen and I were called in to see our OIC, McNary. When we entered his office we found Tom, our platoon LPO (Leading Petty Officer), and Chief Dan there with him. Clearly something was up, something big, but we had no idea what. Were we in some sort of trouble?

"Listen," said McNary, "you guys have done a really great job here, and we're short-handed on snipers right now. We want to offer you the opportunity to go to sniper school."

Of course, we all knew the SEALs had snipers, and we all knew how difficult a course it was. The whole thing seemed fascinating, but I'd never for an instant considered becoming one of those guys. All my life, I'd loved being in the water, and all my life I'd wanted to be a pilot, but a sniper? Not a chance. Yet, now here it was, being offered to us on a plate.

We were stunned. We were thrilled. We were terrified.

•   •   •

It was unheard of for a new guy to get a sniper billet. There were some seriously seasoned guys on the team who had waited years to get a slot. That's how hard they usually were to get. We knew it was a fiendishly difficult school to pass, and the last thing anyone wanted was some wet-behind-the-ears new guy in there, because he'd just mess it up and wash out. We also knew that everyone would be watching us, including our entire platoon—make that our entire team—and that they would all be counting on us. If we washed out, we would be letting them all down. If we said yes, we would spend the next three months under excruciating pressure.

We didn't hesitate for a second.

CHAPTER
TWENTY-EIGHT

There are some pretty difficult schools and training courses in the U.S. military, but none has quite the reputation of SEAL sniper training. It is one of the toughest programs anywhere on the planet.

The course is three months of twelve-plus-hour days, seven days a week. After going through the brutality of BUD/S and some of the programs in STT, there was nothing in the sniper course that posed any real physical challenge. But it is an extremely mentally challenging course.

Don't get me wrong. You have to be physically tough. Sniper training demands that every graduate be one of a unique breed, willing to snake his way through treacherous, urban war-zone terrain or crawl the hot desert floor for hours, slow as a snail and often in his own bodily waste, sometimes withstanding days on end of unendurable physical hardship, to set up on his target.

Still, the physical ability is maybe 10 percent of it. Most of it is mental.

Sniper school is one of the very few courses a SEAL will not be looked down upon for failing to complete. It's an unwritten rule that you don't give guys a hard time for washing out of sniper school. Because the course is known for its insane difficulty, just being selected or volunteering to go automatically elicits respect in the teams.

The students who entered the course were already the cream of the crop, but the dropout rate was still vicious. When I took the sniper course in the spring of 2000, we classed up with twenty-six guys at the start. After three months of continuous training, only twelve of us would graduate.

A few weeks after our conversation in Lieutenant McNary's office, Glen and I, along with two dozen others, mustered for our initial sniper school in-briefing.

There are two principal parts to sniper training. First is the shooting phase, which focuses on learning the weapons, advanced ballistics, and, of course, the actual marksmanship training, during which we would work in pairs taking turns as shooter or spotter. Second is the stalking phase, during which we would train in the arts of stealth and concealment. The course concludes with our graded final training exercise (FTX) out in the California desert near Niland.

We learned we would be conducting the shooting phase at the Coalinga range, a private inland facility about a hundred miles northwest of Bakersfield, California. We would camp out, receive all our instruction, and do all our shooting there.

We were led to the team armory, where we each checked out the suite of weapons we would be working with over the next few months. We each got a sniper M14, a Remington .308 bolt gun, a Remington .300 Win Mag, and a .50 cal, along with scopes and ammo.

Once we had our weapons, we mustered back to meet our instructors.

At the time, a master chief named Jordan ran the sniper school, but he was just in the process of turning it over to Senior Chief Seth Carver. Seth was a total professional and highly respected by everyone there. He was simply one of the good guys, one of those instructors we could count on both for his expertise and for his solid character.

Unfortunately, that didn't apply to all the instructors. In terms of their shooting skills, these guys were all at the top of their game, but they were not necessarily good teachers. This is something we would change later on, when I became part of the team that redesigned the entire sniper course, but when we went through the course back in 2000, there wasn't much emphasis on teaching skills. It was a sink-or-swim deal. Here's the training. If you don't get it, tough.

CHAPTER TWENTY-NINE

Glen and I were happy to learn we had been paired as shooting partners. We had been working together in GOLF platoon for over a year by this point, had developed a good friendship, and trusted each other completely. Now we just had to do the work—and do it perfectly.

We kicked off the course by going out to Camp Pendleton for a qualifying shoot. Just to start the sniper course, we had to be shooting on the standard navy rifle at expert level. They took us through a brief class to make sure we all knew how to set up and operate all our weapons, and then we were out on the range shooting.

We started off at a hundred yards, doing a standing shot, then sitting shot, then standing-to-sitting rapid, then a prone slow fire, then a standing-to-prone rapid fire. Next we went out to two hundred yards and shot another volley. Out of a perfect score of 200, we had to shoot at least 180 to qualify as shooting expert. We each got two tries. We lost a few guys right then and there.

The rest of us saddled up and headed north for Coalinga, where we would spend the next six weeks camping out on the property of the Coalinga Rifle Club, a five-hour drive from San Diego. When we arrived, we found the place had a shower, bathroom facilities, a small kitchen, and that was about it. The classes would take place outdoors on picnic tables under the cover of a few shade trees. As we soon learned, it got wicked hot out there.

This place sports one of the largest shooting ranges in the West. It's also fairly isolated—far enough away from any distractions that it would force us to focus on the task at hand.

A few days after we arrived, guys from the Army Marksman-ship Unit (AMU), the military's elite match shooting team, joined us. The SEALs are not known for their humility within the special operations community, but for what it's worth, we always strive for the best, even when that means going outside our community. In this case, our instructors were smart enough to bring in the best of the best. These guys could shoot.

I quickly realized I needed to pay attention, take notes, and do whatever these guys suggested. This was some of the best marks-manship training I have ever received, and their training methods would not only stay with me throughout my time in the teams, they would also influence my teaching practices in the future.

We started out shooting iron sights, meaning without scopes, on the 7.62mm M14, a classic rifle that the U.S. military had relied on for four decades. Iron sights on a rifle consist of two elements, a rear sight and front sight, which you use to line up your view of the target. They are similar to the little notchlike sights on a pistol, except that the M14 rifle sights provide knobs that allow you to dial in your windage (side-to-side adjustment to compensate for the ef-fects of wind) and elevation (vertical adjustment to compensate for factors including distance).

The AMU sharpshooters taught us the fundamentals, including sight picture and sight alignment, breathing, grip, and trigger pull. They taught us about sight fixture: fixing on that sight post, which may be a centimeter wide on the front sight, visually splitting it in half and focusing on the top center edge. This requires an exceptionally tight degree of mental focus and concentration. A visual misalignment of even a tiny fraction of a millimeter, magnified by the distance you're shooting from, can result in a complete miss, and the farther out you're shooting, the greater that magnification—in other words, the greater the need for complete accuracy in your sight alignment.

They taught us how to control our breath and how to work with our natural breathing cycle. Common sense might suggest that the best way to take an accurate shot would be to hold your breath. Actually, it's just the opposite. Instead of fighting your natural breathing cycle, you have to learn how to use it. When you're lying down, as you typically are when taking aim for a long shot, your rifle's sights slowly rise and fall with the movement of your chest expanding and contracting. What you want to do is time your shot so that it comes precisely during the lull of the natural respiratory pause at the bottom of your exhale, so your breathing doesn't affect the shot's elevation.

They taught us about something called natural point of aim. Whether you're kneeling, sitting, standing, or lying down, after you put your sights on the target, you scoot your body back and forth until you've put yourself into a position where you're naturally aligned with the target. If you have to swing your arm over to get on sight with the target, even if only slightly, that means you are using your muscles, which is not ideal. Instead, you want to be relaxed in perfect position such that your alignment is naturally focused on the target.

We shot all the way back to eight hundred yards without scopes, except for a personal spotting scope. We would have the spotting scope set up next to us so we could lean over, look through the scope, read the wind (for both direction and wind speed) and the mirage, estimate the windage in minutes of angle (a minute is one-sixtieth of a degree), dial in a correction on our iron sight windage knob, then roll over and take the shot. Mirage is the heat-rippling effect you see when you look down a highway on a hot day. You can adjust your scope so it's visible, and it flows like a river, either to the right or to the left, showing which way the wind is blowing. Or it might flow straight upward, in which case we call it a boil, meaning that there is either no wind at all or that the wind is blowing straight toward you.

You're also looking for any telltale signs, whether it's grass blowing in the distance or just the feel of the wind on your face. You get to be an acute observer of exactly what is going on in your environment and an excellent judge of how to apply that to your weapon.

There is a tremendous amount of science involved in making all these observations, but the art of it is bringing them all together into an extremely precise picture of the overall scenario. What is the weather doing at your position as the shooter? Looking down the range halfway to your target, what's happening at that position? Is that valley funneling the wind a certain way? What's happening eight hundred yards away, all the way down to where the target is sitting? Is the wind calm there, or moving, and if so, in what direction, and how strongly? Calculating all those factors, then assembling them all together to arrive at an estimation of exactly what you think is happening and precisely how it all applies to your weapon, and then making the perfect shot—it's incredibly complicated. And there is zero margin for error.

CHAPTER THIRTY

During the day we shot for five hours in the morning, then received instruction and testing until dark, went to sleep, woke up, and did it all over again.

In our second week on the M14 iron sights we started shooting cold bore tests every morning at 6:00 A.M., and the stress levels escalated.

The cold bore shot is staged to simulate that all-important first shot taken in a combat situation in the field, when you don't have the luxury of taking practice shots and letting your rifle warm up. You need to be able to sight down a cold gun and take that first shot, right out of the box, with 100 percent reliable accuracy. That first shot has to be a kill shot—because if it isn't, you likely won't get a second chance.

The unique conditions of a cold bore shot are not simply a matter of human factors. Yes, that's part of it. We had to learn how to be at the top of our game instantly, with no opportunity to warm up and shake it out with a few practice shots. But there's also pure physics involved, because the bullet behaves very differently when the rifle is cold. As you shoot rounds through a metal chamber, it heats up, creating an increase in chamber pressure, which translates into a change in the bullet's trajectory. Put a bullet through a hot chamber and it may travel as much as a few hundred feet per second faster than when you put it through a cold chamber. Elevation—how far the bullet travels before giving in to gravity and beginning its downward arc—is profoundly affected. This is why snipers are careful to track and log our cold bore data.

The night before, they would tell us, "Tomorrow morning, the whole class on the five-hundred-yard line"—or whatever point on the range they'd selected. I would go to sleep with my single bullet next to me in my sleeping bag and my gun and kit all laid out and ready to go.

We awoke early to head out to the range, taking only our rifle and a single round. Once we assembled at the designated location, they gave us our instructions: "Okay, you've got thirty seconds to sprint to the three-hundred-yard line and engage your target from the standing position. Ready, go." We took off at a sprint.

Right away, we were dealing with conflicting parameters. The faster you run, the sooner you get to your location and the more time you have to line up the shot—but the faster you run, the harder it is to control your breathing once you get there, which means the greater the chance that your breathing will mess up your shot. In those thirty seconds you not only have to reach your location, you also then have to read the wind correctly, dial in the dope (the correct elevation data), identify your own target (nothing worse than shooting someone else's!), estimate lead if yours happens to be a moving target, do your best to slow down your heart rate, and in general get yourself together as rapidly as is humanly possible.

Then you take the shot.

There were a lot of ways to mess this up. Sometimes guys would forget to put their round in the chamber, or forget to dial in the right elevation. If we were starting out on the five-hundred-yard line, for example, we would have already dialed that into our sights when we got there. But, if we then sprinted to the three-hundred-yard line and forgot to dial elevation down to three hundred, we'd miss the shot. Sometimes guys would get everything right but be so nervous about forgetting something they would just blow the shot anyway.

The cold bore test was scored on a 10-point scale. If your shot landed inside the kill zone of the human silhouette on the target (head and heart), you received a 10. If you shot outside the kill zone but still within the human silhouette, you got an 8. Miss the silhouette but still manage to hit the target and you scored a 7. If you missed the target altogether you landed a 0. And the other guys would then avoid you like the plague for fear your bad juju would rub off. Two or three goose eggs bought you a one-way ticket back to your SEAL team. This was made crystal clear to us from the beginning.

The standard to beat was 80 percent, and if you didn't at least meet that standard, there was no drama about it, you were just gone. You made the cut, or you were out. I saw guys whose scores came in at 79 percent told to pack their bags. Every day was survival. As the saying goes in the teams, "The only easy day was yesterday."

Another part of the cold bore routine was edge shots. We would lie down in our lane and wait for the target, which would suddenly appear at some point in the next twenty minutes. We would have no idea when it was coming. All we could do was wait in a state of total vigilance. Take your eyes off the sight for even a moment, to wipe sweat off your brow, scratch an itch on your face, or take a drink of water, and you could miss it entirely.

The cold bore shot was one of the most stressful events of the entire day. Hit or miss, that shot would stay with you. Make a good shot and you were a hero. Blow it and your own personal dark cloud hung over your head for the rest of the day.

CHAPTER THIRTY-ONE

I'll never forget the morning of my first cold bore shot. We ran out onto the range, got our instructions, hustled to our shooting line, threw ourselves on the ground, and scrambled mightily to get it together for that first shot.

"One!"

"Two!"

"Three!"

"Four!"

One by one we counted off our lane numbers, right to left, so that we knew for sure which lane we were shooting in and wouldn't mess up and hit someone else's target. I chambered my one and only round, got myself settled into my natural point of aim as best I could, target aligned and on sights, felt the tide of my respiration ebb to its lowest point, and in the short moment of that stillness I squeezed the trigger—and missed the target completely.

Oh, man, I thought. Right off the bat, I was in the hole: a 0. I couldn't afford many more of those if I hoped to survive.

Fortunately for me, that was my first and only complete miss. I started out pretty rough in the cold bore tests, hitting mostly 7s. As the days went by, I steadily improved my ability to control myself, and my scores slowly crept upward.

The stress of that morning cold bore shot got to a number of guys in the class. Sometimes they just could not bring the day's score up to 80 percent. Pretty soon the camp started thinning out as our numbers began to dwindle.

The cold bore shot felt to me like the perfect expression of what it means to be a SEAL sniper, and it carried over into everything we did. We quickly learned that you can't always have the ideal circumstances, or even reasonably helpful circumstances. You can't always take practice shots. You have to be ready to perform at the very top of your abilities, instantly and without preparation, and under the very worst of circumstances—and do it over and over again. Perfectly. Every time.

CHAPTER THIRTY-TWO

During our long hours on the range, we were not shooting the entire time. They would split the class in half, and while one half was shooting, the other half was down in the butts, pulling and marking targets for our classmates.

The butts was a secured bunker area behind the targets that provided a little shade and held the large target frames. When we rotated to the butts, we would be in charge of raising and lowering the target frames on a pulley system in order to mark the bullet impacts and clean them off in preparation for the next round.

The shooting drills kept us busy for up to eight hours a day. We also had extensive classroom work, which we did mostly during the heat of the day, sandwiched in between sessions on the range.

Every few classes we would be tested on whatever we'd learned. As with the shooting tests, it was either pass or you're gone.

One of our classes consisted of a series of drills called keep-in-memory exercises, or KIMs. As a sniper, there are times when you have only a brief glance at a situation, and you have to be able to fix it all in your memory almost instantaneously. These exercises were designed to hone our capacity for accurate snapshot memory.

The instructors would lay a tarp over an array of objects, bring us in, yank off the tarp, and give us thirty seconds to look at and memorize everything. Then the tarp went back on everything and we'd have to write down everything we saw and remembered.

Sometimes they would scatter a series of objects over a hillside. We'd have to scan it quickly with our binoculars and in that brief glance pick out everything that was out of the ordinary.

We also did very detailed target sketches, similar to the KIMs. In a given amount of time, we would have to sketch a target in detail and also record all sorts of data. From which direction was the sun shining? What were the weather patterns? Where were possible helo insertion points? Helo extraction points? Exactly what was happening right around the area of the target? Digital cameras and laptops were not used as commonly as they are today, so we had to do our field sketches and recording of information by hand.

Some of our most extensive classroom study was in the area of ballistics, including internal and external ballistics.

Internal ballistics is what's happening on the inside of the rifle. When your firing pin hits the bullet's strike plate, it sets off an initial powder charge. The exploding powder creates a rapidly expanding gas bubble, which propels the slug, or front portion of the bullet, through the chamber. It's very much a miniature version of a rocket ship launch. Just as the rocket discards its boosters once it's in flight, the rifle ejects the empty cartridge, sending only the relatively small front portion on its journey. In the rocket's case, that's the capsule that houses the astronauts. In the bullet's case, it's the death-dealing slug.

The inside of the rifle's barrel is inscribed with a series of spiral grooves, or rifling (where the term "rifle" comes from). This puts a fast spin on the bullet, giving it stability in flight, much the way you put a spin on a football when you throw it. Internal ballistics has to do with how many twists there are in the barrel and their precise effect on the bullet, how fast the bullet travels, and how it's moving when it exits the rifle.

This is where external ballistics takes over. Your bullet will start its journey at a velocity of over two thousand feet per second. However, the moment it emerges from the barrel its flight path is already being influenced by its environment. Leaving aside for the moment the effect of wind, there is a universal drag created by the friction of that ocean of air the bullet pierces through in order to fly, combined with the downward pull of gravity. At a certain distance, different for different weapons and ammunition, your particular rifle bullet slows to the point where it passes from supersonic to subsonic. As it eats through the yards at rates of something like one yard every one one-thousandth of a second, the integrity of its flight path becomes compromised. A .308 bullet traveling at 2,200 feet per second will lose its flight path stability to the point where it starts tumbling head over heels by about 900 or 1,000 meters out.

External ballistics is also about exactly what that flight path looks like. When you shoot a .308 at a target eight hundred yards away, you're not shooting in a straight line. The bullet actually makes a pretty big arc. Imagine throwing a football from the fifty-yard line to the end zone. You don't throw it straight toward the goal. Instead, you have to throw it upward so that it arcs through the air, hitting its high point at about the twenty-five-yard line and then curving back down to reach the end zone. The same thing happens with the .308 bullet. You're not shooting it in a straight line; you're really throwing it up in the air so that it arcs and comes down where you want it to. Understanding exactly how that works can have a make-or-break bearing on you hitting your target.

For example, let's say you're shooting at something eight hundred yards away. In the terrain lying between you and your target, you notice a low-hanging bridge. From all appearances, that's no problem. Your target stands at maybe five-foot-eight. You are lying

on the ground, on your stomach. The bridge is a good ten feet off
the ground at its lowest point. When you sight down through your
scope at the target, you can see a clear pathway from you straight
to the target. No problem, right?

Wrong. That bridge may not look like it's in the way—but when
you take into account the arc your bullet needs to travel to land at
your projected site, that bridge could be lying directly in the path
of what we call the bullet's top arc. In other words, it could stop
your bullet cold, halfway to your target. And in the kinds of circumstances a sniper often faces, you will not have the luxury of a
second shot. You have to know your bullet's maximum ordinate—
that is, the maximum height that bullet will reach on its path to your
target, and calculate for that.

CHAPTER THIRTY-THREE

Once we had mastered the M14 we moved on to other weapons, starting with the .308 bolt-action Remington, a very solid weapon and quite capable, in the right hands, out to eight hundred or nine hundred yards. This was our first look at a real scoped weapon—and right away, I knew I had a problem. There was a Leupold scope on one of my guns that just didn't seem quite right. I pretty quickly realized that it wasn't maintaining at zero. It was slipping off. There was no way I could shoot with a scope that wasn't reliable.

These weapons are not delicate; they're made to withstand the rigors of combat. However, they are pieces of precision machinery, and they're not infallible. For example, the barrel of a .300 Win Mag is only good for a few thousand rounds, and then you shoot out the barrel and it starts losing accuracy. We were shooting thousands and thousands of rounds.

If your gun starts to malfunction in the middle of a shooting evolution, the instructor might assume it's you.

In a lot of cases, he's right. In some cases, though, the weapon really is shot out, or there's some kind of equipment malfunction. We had a few guys who were excellent shots but got flushed out of the course because they had the bad luck of getting a weapon that didn't have a good log and was legitimately shot out, and they didn't yet have the skills or know-how to deal with it right away.

I was determined not to let that happen. My first shooting test was coming up. No way was this faulty scope going to flush me from sniper school. I told my instructors about it, and when they didn't do anything I kept bringing it up. I wouldn't let it rest. Finally they got an armorer out there from the navy's ordnance testing division. He looked at the scope and said, "Yeah, you have a bad optic."

What a relief. I easily could have flunked out in my first test because of a messed-up scope.

At the same time that we started working with scopes on the .308, we also started working in pairs, taking turns as shooter and spotter. The shooter's job is to put everything else out of his mind, take the information the spotter feeds him, and make a perfect shot, period. As we soon learned, the spotter's job is in many ways more complex and more difficult.

As spotter, you are on the spotting scope, identifying and monitoring the target. Your job is to calculate windage and give target lead if necessary (that is, how much to compensate for the target's movement). As spotter you also watch the shot trace, which tells its own story and either proves the call dead-on accurate or gives important clues for correcting the next shot. Yes, even though it is traveling at speeds of two thousand feet per second or more, you actually watch the thing. In most cases you can literally see those vapor trails all the way in to the target.

The spotter has to consider all these things—and you had to learn it all in a hurry, or you would be going home.

Even aside from the fact that we were friends, Glen and I soon found that we made an excellent sniper pair. Glen is a naturally gifted marksman. I don't remember him ever missing a single shot, and most of his shots were perfect tens. For my part, I seemed to have a natural gift for reading the wind and being able to calculate all the conditions and circumstances. I think this had to do with my experiences with navigation and having grown up near the water. Water currents and wind currents may be two very different things, but the same basic concepts apply to them both.

Soon we had our first graded test on the .308. As pairs we shared a combined grade, so we knew we would sink or swim together as a shooter-spotter pair. Glen and I scored in the nineties on that first test, but by that time we were both feeling completely frazzled and harried.

Still, we knew we had developed into a solid shooting pair, and we seemed to handle the stress better than many of the other guys. During that first paired shooting evolution, we could see the tension level in some of the other pairs simmering. By the time of that test, a few of them went through complete meltdowns.

Pretty soon it dawned on us that the steadily escalating stress we were seeing was being carefully orchestrated by the instructors. They were constantly watching and testing us to see who could handle the stress and who could not.

One day, while I was spotting, Glen took a shot that I could clearly see had struck the target—but our instructor marked it as a miss.

We continued on with the evolution unfazed. Later we learned that the instructor had called down to the butts over the radio and told the students who were working our lane to mark his hit as a miss. Why? Just to mess with us and see how we would handle it.

We were fortunate. By this time Glen had developed total faith in my spotting, making us killing machines on the range—and we had already realized that the instructors were playing games with us to see how well we handled adverse situations. Some guys didn't get this, and they would self-destruct.

They gave us two kinds of tests on the .308, starting with a snaps and movers test. Snaps and movers involves targets that suddenly appear out of nowhere, snapping upright in a variety of locations and at different, unpredictable time intervals, and targets that move continuously, left and right, in random and unpredictable order. These are full-size E-silhouette targets, a flat panel with a sort of bottle-shaped silhouette on it that represents a human torso and head. Typically we had three head snaps and three moving targets on each yard line, positioned at the two-hundred-, four-hundred-, six-hundred-, and eight-hundred-yard lines.

Working with snaps and movers was where we learned how to lead a moving target. This is tricky, because you have to take into account what the wind is doing and calculate for the distance that you have to lead ahead of the target as it moves. It can feel counterintuitive at first, because often you shouldn't aim where common sense tells you that you ought be aiming.

I remember the first time I put my crosshairs directly on the target, even though it was obviously not stationary and everything in me was screaming at me to move the crosshairs a few degrees off in the direction the target was moving—in other words, to lead the target. According to what we were learning, however, the wind would push my bullet out of its attempted straight path and, over the course of its arc toward the target, actually blow it into the target and cancel out those few degrees of lead. If this sounds like some kind of bizarre funhouse-mirror maze of calculations and competing factors, that's exactly what it felt like—and it all had to happen on a time scale of thousandths of a second. It felt completely wrong, but the logic of external ballistics told me it was right on the money.

I squeezed the trigger and ping! The target went down.

Next was an unknown distance test. For this, they laid out a series of steel targets in each lane at various elevations and distances unknown to us, all the way from fifty to nine hundred yards, which was right at the outer limit of effective range for the .308. This was where we started really learning how to use our scopes and, in particular, figure out range estimation using the mil dot scope reticle.

The reticle, or crosshairs, in a sniper rifle scope is outfitted with two series of tiny dots, called mil dots, that run horizontally and vertically through the field of vision and allow us to measure the approximate height and width of sighted objects by making some simple visual calculations.

If we saw that our target measured, say, 1.5 mil in height in the scope, and we knew the target's actual height in inches, then we could plug that into a formula that would give us the target's distance. As long as we had a known measurement to work with, we could work out the exact range. Practically any kind of known measurement would do. We learned to ask questions like "What's the standard dimension of a Middle Eastern license plate? What's the height and dimension of a standard stop sign in the Middle East? What's the standard window height?" We learned to record this information carefully, knowing that sooner or later, we would be in a situation in some Middle Eastern country and need to know how to calculate the range of a target so we could dial in the correct elevation before taking the shot—and do it fast.

We also have laser rangefinders, of course, which give us these measurements directly, but in the sniper course we had to learn how to make these calculations the hard way. To tell the truth, even with all the new technology, it's still smart to know how to do this by hand. You don't want to count on always having a laser rangefinder handy.

We practiced ranging these targets, and once we ranged them we shot to verify that we had ranged correctly. Then we'd make slight modifications, if necessary, and shoot again. We had ample opportunity to perfect the process in practice tests, but when the final test day came, it was game on and no second chances.

After we spent weeks practicing and testing with the .308, they put us on the .300 Win Mag, which packs more power than the .308 and can therefore shoot to ranges up to a thousand yards and beyond. Each of these has its own characteristics, and by the time the shooting phase was over we had come to know them both like old friends.

We also started doing some longer-distance shooting with the .50-cal sniper rifle. The .50-cal bullet is a monster, about twice the size of the .308, and it can shoot way out past a thousand yards to as much as eighteen hundred yards. It's also a more stable bullet with a little more powder and oomph behind it, and it serves more as what we call an area weapon, meaning that we would typically use it for things like shooting out an engine block in a vehicle or the propeller system in a Scud missile.

And here something strange happened. When we started getting out to certain distances with the .50 cal, we started seeing effects we just didn't understand. We were shooting out to fifteen hundred yards, shooting at tanks and other big targets, and I wondered, *How come I'm holding for a ten-mph wind that's coming in from the right, but the bullet's still not on target—and I can see the trace doing something weird? What is going on?*

What was going on, I eventually learned, was something called the Coriolis effect. This refers to the influence of the Earth's rotation on bodies in motion. Yes, incredibly enough, on top of all the other environmental and ballistic information a sniper keeps in his head, the Earth's rotation is yet one more factor to bear in mind.

Here's why. While my .50-cal bullet was in the air, the Earth's rotation would cause the planet's surface and everything on it—including my target—to slip slightly eastward, so that by the time the bullet landed, nothing was exactly where it had been when that bullet's flight began. Because the Earth is so large and the local impact of its rotation so subtle, it's practically impossible to detect this without scientific instruments, until you start looking at motion over large distances—like fifteen hundred yards.

Shooting out to two hundred, five hundred, even eight hundred or a thousand yards, the impact of the Coriolis effect is so negligible that you can get away with ignoring it. Once you're shooting out to some serious distances, though, it can move your bullet's trajectory by as much as several inches, enough to cause you to completely miss your target.

It was all such a massive amount of information to take in, and I soon learned to use my brain as a lens to bring that entire universe of variables to bear on the tiny circle of focus inside my scope. This also meant blocking out any distractions, such as when the instructors intentionally messed with us to get us flustered and throw us off our game. Or when our own fears about not passing the course crept up on us. We had to just pour every atom of concentration into that focal point.

We had learned to use the PEQ laser sight that projects a visible red dot on the target. That red dot came to represent everything I was learning, compressed into a pinpoint of brilliant light.

It was as if I were standing inside a minuscule red circle, hurling the bullet to its destination by an act of sheer mental concentration. In those moments on the range, everything else disappeared and my world shrank, like the near-infinite compression of matter in a black hole, into that red circle.

CHAPTER THIRTY-FOUR

The more we learned, practiced, and tested, the more grueling it got. Our classmates dropped away, one by one. Finally six weeks had gone by and it was time for our final test.

The test was a combination of snaps and movers and unknown distance. Again, as a sniper team, Glen and I not only took every test together, we also combined our individual grades so that we were graded as a team, not as individuals.

On the .300 Win Mag snaps and movers, we did well, both shooting into the 90s. Then we moved to the unknown distance.

I went first. We ranged the targets. Then it was time for me to shoot. We had a time limit of twenty minutes for this part of the test, and it was the spotter's responsibility to keep track of time and keep us moving it along. But we started having some trouble. Glen was experiencing a little bit of difficulty reading the wind and putting me on the target.

We were on our third lane, with two more lanes to go, when I got an uneasy sense that we were running out of time. I let it go and put all my focus on the next target. Suddenly the test instructor called out, "Time!"

I stared at Glen. "What?" I had eight bullets and two lanes' worth of targets left.

Glen stared at his watch, devastated. "Dude, I don't know what happened."

I was furious—not at Glen, because I knew there was no way he would have intentionally messed this up, but I was stunned. To this day, I don't know what went wrong. But whatever it was, it had happened, and I had scored something like a 60.

Fortunately for us, we had hit every target, so we hadn't dropped any rounds. And, because we were combining our grades, we still had a chance. Now it was Glen's turn to shoot and my turn to spot, which meant we were both about to play to our strengths.

"Okay, listen," I said, "we have to get you a score of 95 or higher." That would net us a combined score that would squeak us by on this test. It meant Glen could miss one shot, and only one shot. The rest would have to be perfect 100s. This was our last test before leaving the range and moving on to the stalking phase—if we did move on, that is. If we didn't score a 95 or higher on Glen's shoot, then at least one of us would not be going on to the stalking phase. Glen might or might not be out, but I definitely would be history.

Meanwhile, Glen was still beating himself up.

"Dude," I said, "we need to let this go. We need to clean this test. Let's just do this thing."

So we did. Ignoring the instructor's wicked chuckling, we switched places and slid over to the next lane. I was like a machine, calling that wind. I put him on every shot, and he took every shot. We both put everything else out of our minds, climbed into that red circle, and put ourselves on the top of our game. Glen shot a 95. When they did the scoring, Glen had tied another guy, Mike Bearden, for the highest score of the day.

CHAPTER THIRTY-FIVE

Having cleared the hurdles of the shooting phase, we headed off to the Niland desert for the second half of the sniper course, the stalking phase. Now that we had all these skills on the gun, it was time to train us in the arts of camouflage and stealth so that we could with 100 percent consistency and reliability place ourselves in the necessary position to use those gun skills. It doesn't matter how good a shot you are if you can't get close enough to take the shot in the first place.

Classes on stealth and movement came first. We learned how to use natural vegetation to our advantage, especially in outfitting our ghillie suits. A ghillie suit starts out as a base outfit with a neutral desert pattern. Then you clip on scraps of vegetation growing in the immediate environment. For our ghillie suits, we also used scraps of burlap in different shades, which we learned to vary depending on the specific environment in which we'd be stalking.

This sounds simple, but it is amazing to see the

degree to which this art can be perfected. When you look at a photo of a Navy SEAL sniper in a ghillie suit out in his environment, it's almost like looking at one of those "hidden pictures." You look and look, but all you can see is trees and bushes. The sniper blends in completely.

They taught us how to make a veg fan, clipping branches from manzanita bushes or whatever happened to be around and zip-tying them together. We learned how to hide behind and use this improvised camouflage. We would slowly rise up in the middle of it, peeking over the top of the fan, using either our binos or the naked eye to get an idea of where our target was. Then we'd slowly melt back down again.

They taught us how to use what they called dead space, which proved to be one of our most important lessons. Imagine standing on the street, next to a car at the curb. If someone is looking in your direction from the sidewalk and you crouch down below the back of the car, suddenly you disappear. You're using the dead space of the car to cover your signature. You can do the same thing with bushes, boulders, even a few feet of rising or sinking elevation, like a dirt mound or shallow ditch—anything you can put between you and your target.

The terrain in Niland didn't provide much in the way of natural cover. It's pretty flat, desolate scenery. But even there in that cracked-earth desert, you can find dead space if you look for it. There are tumbleweeds and other desert bushes, slight dips and rises in elevation, rocks here and there, even an occasional scraggly tree. Find even a little gully, and if you can slip down in there, you've got dead space.

They also taught us how to camouflage our rifles when setting up in our final firing position (FFP), and how to make sure we had cleared the muzzle by tamping down the firing area or using veg clippers to clip away vegetation surrounding the muzzle, so that when we took that shot, the pressure wave wouldn't cause any movement in nearby trees or grass. The last thing you want to do is take a shot and have it create a big signature. Even if you are completely hidden and unseen when you take the shot, if someone whips around and looks to see where that sound came from and sees some grasses swaying or branches moving, he might make your position and nail you.

We also practiced building hide sites. We would dig into the ground, sometimes using mesh or chicken wire we'd brought with us, but mostly using whatever natural terrain we might find on-site. It was almost like becoming a burrowing animal. In the desert, especially, a hide site provides not only cover but also a bit of relief from the intense heat. If you build it right, someone can be standing right next to you and never even realize you're there. You might have four guys living in this thing for days on end, watching the target, radioing back to base until they give you authority to take the shot.

Then we started stalking drills. They take you out to some desert location and say, "Your target is two to four kilometers in that direction. You've got two hours to get to within 180 to 220 yards of it, set up, and take your shot."

Off you go, crawling on your belly, you and your gun and your drag bag, which you've hooked to your belt and now drag along behind you, inching along in the sweltering heat. A half hour goes by, then an hour. Some guys around you go to the bathroom in their ghillie suits. What else are they going to do? You have to get within that range—and you aren't allowed to use laser rangefinders, so you have to use your scope to measure your target and then figure out exactly what point you have to reach in order to be within about two hundred yards.

Two instructors are waiting for you in the command tower, scouring the area with their high-powered binos, looking for you and communicating by radio with three or four walkers on the ground. The walkers are instructors who walk the field. They are not there to hunt you but to carry out commands from the tower. If an instructor detects movement, he'll radio the walker who is nearest to that spot and direct him over to it. If and when that walker is standing right next to you, he says, "Roger that." You're busted. You've failed the stalk.

The whole idea is to make this as difficult as possible. By the time you are in firing position, you're only about two hundred yards from the tower. You're up against two trained sniper instructors who know exactly what direction you're coming from, know exactly what area you have to set up in, and who have not only high-powered binos but also a laser rangefinder. They know you're coming and would love nothing more than to bust you.

If you've made it this far, now comes the moment of painstaking patience, as you slowly pull out your gun, then pull out your scope, and get everything into place. You can't let your scope give off any kind of reflection or glint of sunlight, so you might cover it with fine mesh, then slowly move into position, get your sight positioned on the target, and squeeze off your shot.

For that first shot, you shoot a blank, which essentially announces that you have made it to your FFP. The walker approaches to within three feet of you, then signals the two instructors in the tower that he is in your vicinity. The instructors take a look, peering in your direction with their high-powered binos. If they see you, you fail. If they aren't able to see you, then they get on the radio to the walker and say, "Okay, give him his bullet."

Now they turn away for a moment, so they can't see the walker come up and hand you your live cartridge. They set up a target right where they had been sitting moments earlier, and clear out. Now you take your shot and hit the target—you hope.

There's a lot that can go wrong. If your bullet path isn't completely clear and your bullet even lightly grazes a small twig or branch as it hurtles through the air that can easily be enough to throw its trajectory off and result in a complete miss. And you're lying down, remember. There might be a small mound of dirt in the way that you hadn't noticed.

If you do everything right and hit that target on the chest or the head, you score a 10. Hit just anywhere else inside the silhouette, and you score a 9; just hitting the target scores you an 8. Miss, and you've earned a 0.

Then you get up, walk back to the truck, and wait for everyone else. And by the way, after you take that shot you better not leave a trace. We had guys who stalked all the way into position and got off a very decent shot but then left behind a piece of brass, a zip tie, or a veg clipper. They failed the stalk.

We started doing several stalks a day, the two- to four-kilometer one in the morning, and then a one-kilometer stalk in the evening. We would practice for a few days and then be tested.

My first stalk, I ran out of time before I even got to my FFP. It was humiliating. I made up my mind, right then and there, that that was not going to happen again.

I quickly learned that the first priority was to get eyes on the target. Once you have eyes on the target, then you own it. You know exactly where the enemy is, but he doesn't know where you are. From that vantage point, you can set about planning your exact route to your FFP.

Jack Nicklaus, the legendary championship golfer, used to say that when you're making a difficult shot, 50 percent of it is the mental picture you create, 40 percent is how you set it up, and 10 percent is the swing itself. In that respect, sniping is a lot like golf: 90 percent of it is how you see the picture and get your shot lined up.

I realized that a lot of the other guys were getting down on the ground and just taking off, crawling in the general direction of the tower without first having gotten eyes on the target. As a consequence, they wouldn't really know exactly where it was they were going, and they would run out of time—just like I did.

For my second stalk I figured, *Hey, this is practice—let's push the limits and see what happens.*

Instead of getting down on the ground, I set off at a bold stride in the direction the instructors had told us the target was located. I passed guys who were crawling on their bellies on the hot Niland ground, slowly and painfully, and they looked up at me bug-eyed, with expressions that said, what are you doing? I figured there was no way the instructors would see me; I was still almost half a mile away, and besides, they wouldn't be really looking yet, because they wouldn't be expecting any of us to start getting close nearly that soon.

I kept going until I had eyes on the target—and then immediately got down into a low crouch and started checking out every detail about the terrain between the target and me. Once I had my route planned, I got down on my belly and started crawling the three hundred yards or so I still needed to cover in order to get to my FFP. Moving as quickly and as stealthily as I could, it took me maybe thirty minutes to low-crawl into position, set up my firing point, get everything dialed in, and go.

From that point on, it started to click for me. I would find a little high ground and make sure I had eyes on the target, and as soon as I knew exactly where it was, I would map out my approach, put a big terrain feature between me and the target, and then just walk right up on it. I started taking down 10s, perfect stalks every time.

Again, I think it was all the time I spent spearfishing. The thing that clicked for me was the concept of dead space. That was the key to these stalking exercises. Put that dead space between you and your targets, and you can literally run up to them without them ever knowing you're there. Although you could hardly come up with a greater contrast in environments than underwater versus the Niland desert, that didn't matter. The concept was exactly the same. Find the dead space and use it.

CHAPTER THIRTY-SIX

I helped a few classmates who were having a hard time getting the hang of it. We were coming down to the very last stalk, and there were three guys who had racked enough poor scores that they now needed to get a perfect score, or else they wouldn't pass. All this time and effort, and it was coming down to this one last stalk that would decide whether or not they would become SEAL snipers. The level of tension was off the charts.

These were really good guys, and I badly wanted all three of them to make it. On our last stalk before the final test, I went with them, doing everything I could to help them get themselves a clean, fast pathway into the zone for a solid FFP. In the process, I didn't pay enough attention to what I was doing myself and hung myself out a little too far. I got busted—and failed the stalk. I didn't mind, though. I had enough margin in my accumulated scores to make it through even with a 0 on that one.

When the final test came, two of them made it. The third went home.

We left Niland and headed back to Coronado to take some brief instruction in how to waterproof our weapons and take care of them when going in and out of the water. After graduation we would spend another week doing two-man contact drills and over-the-beach training, but for all practical purposes, we were done. We'd made it.

The graduation ceremony took place on June 12, 2000, my twenty-sixth birthday. It was a proud moment for everyone in GOLF platoon. Our personal triumph also translated into bragging rights for them and enhanced the reputation of the whole team. Glen and I were on Cloud Nine.

My SEAL sniper certificate carries the signature of Captain William McRaven, who at the time was serving as commander of Naval Special Warfare Group One. More than a decade later, now a four-star admiral, McRaven would be credited with organizing and executing Operation Neptune's Spear, the special ops mission that took out Osama bin Laden in May 2011. The following month he was confirmed as the ninth commander of SOCOM, the entire U.S. Special Operations Command, taking the reins from Admiral Eric T. Olson, another Navy SEAL.

I graduated almost ten years to the day since my dad had thrown me off our family's boat in the South Pacific. Then, I'd been a scared sixteen-year-old kid. Today, I was a Navy SEAL sniper.

PART FIVE

DUTY CALLS

At thirteen with my catch, a ten-pound lobster.

At sixteen on Captain Bill's dive boat, the *Peace*, with a nice Calico bass.

Boat crews in BUD/S. *(I'm on far R.)*

The O-course cargo net, BUD/S First Phase, class 215.

Hell Week in BUD/S First Phase. Notice the telephone poles used for log PT.

My first "stacked duck"—two Zodiacs tied together with G-12 parachutes, about to be tossed out of a plane.

I am a new guy on exercises in Niland with an M-60 machine gun and 1,000 rounds.

GOLF platoon in Niland. *(I'm third from R.)*

With my sniper partner Glen Doherty, getting ready for a 1.5-mile swim one recent summer.

My graduating sniper school class. *(Front row: I am third from L; back row: Mike "Bear" Bearden, second from L; Glen Doherty, fourth from L.)*

ECHO platoon doing perimeter patrol on the USS *Cole*. Notice the ship's gaping wound, dead center.

ECHO platoon patch that I designed in late 2001.

Taking prisoners: Our nighttime takedown on the Persian Gulf.

Kandahar, Afghanistan.

Meeting up with a group of indigenous "friendlies" outside Kandahar.

With two "friendlies."

ECHO platoon in one of the Task Force K-Bar compounds at Kandahar Airport. *(Front row standing: Osman and I on L, Lt. Cassidy second from R.)*

Processing incoming POWs at EPW camp at Kandahar.

Tarnak Farms: On this exact spot a SEAL was later killed by a land mine. *(I'm on the R.)*

Contraband found in the caves at Zhawar Kili; mostly ammo (a mix of American, British, and Russian).

More contraband found in the Zhawar Kili cave complex.

Zhawar Kili: an Al Qaeda recruiting poster (created pre-9/11).

Weapons cache found at Zhawar Kili; notice the debris spread everywhere from air strikes.

Cooking chickens at the deserted village that ECHO platoon used as base of operations in Zhawar Kili. *(L to R: Osman, I, Chief Dye.)*

Destroying a weapons site in the Zhawar Kili area.

Demolition at Zhawar Kili.

ECHO platoon at Bagram Air Base, after returning from Zhawar Kili. *(Back row: Lt. Cassidy, tenth from L; Chief Dye, eleventh from L, Osman twelfth from L; front row: I am fifth from L.)*

ECHO platoon at Kandahar, after the Zhawar Kili mission, with JDAM our mascot. *(With Lt. Cassidy, front row, fourth from L.)*

Lt. Cassidy scanning the area at Prata Ghar.

Major Mike *(far R)*, our German brothers' OIC.

At Kandahar, before the Prata Ghar mission. *(Back row from L: Lt. Cassidy and I; front row on L: Heath Robinson.)*

Ahmed Kheyl exfil; the red smoke is a marker so the exfil helo can see both our location and ground wind direction.

With two German KSK buddies, flying the Afghan colors at Ahmed Kheyl checkpoint.

A moment of silence at Bagram: commemoration for our fallen brothers immediately after the Roberts Ridge incident.

Instructing a sniper school class on the basics of stealth and concealment.

Sniper setting up for a shot at 200 yards from the target in the distance.

Sniper students in the stalking and concealment phase of training.

SEALs conducting a
Gas and Oil Platform
(GOPLAT) takedown.

In Iraq, supporting
"the Client" in urban
intelligence operations.

CHAPTER THIRTY-SEVEN

In the late summer of 2000 our platoon headed for the Persian Gulf by way of Hawaii, Australia, and other points west. My first deployment as a Navy SEAL sniper. We were attached to the USS *Duluth*, a troop transport ship.

Going into that fall, there was no significant conflict for our military forces to focus on. Still, the whole Mideast region was a political and military powder keg that loomed in the background. At the time, SEAL Team Three was involved in reinforcing United Nations economic sanctions against Iraq. Iraq's leader, Saddam Hussein, was having an awful lot of oil smuggled out of the country and sold for high prices. We were expecting to participate in policing the area, which would mean doing a significant number of ship boardings on tankers. Our job would be to catch up with these tankers and stop them before they reached Iranian waters, where American and other NATO personnel could not legally pursue them.

•   •   •

It was October 12, 2000. We had just gotten back onboard the *Duluth* in Bahrain. We were mobilizing to get our equipment and go participate in that ship-boarding detail when we suddenly got word that an American destroyer, the USS *Cole*, had been hit in the nearby Gulf of Aden just off the coast of Yemen, and hit bad.

That morning, the *Cole* had put in at about 9:30 local time for a routine refueling stop. By 10:30 refueling had commenced. At 11:18 a small craft loaded with about a quarter ton of homemade explosives and manned by two individuals approached the ship's port side and made contact. The explosion killed seventeen sailors and injured thirty-nine others of a crew of nearly three hundred, putting a forty-by-forty-foot hole in the hull in the process.

Wait—what? Two guys in a speedboat? How had that happened?

To much of the world, September 11, 2001, was and still is "the day everything changed," and it's easy to understand why. But not for me. For me, everything changed on this day, eleven months earlier.

CHAPTER THIRTY-EIGHT

We took off and were on-site within shooting distance of the Yemeni coast within eight hours, putting our fast boats over the side. The marines had an outfit in Bahrain they called the Fast Company, and they earned their nickname: they were on the scene a few hours ahead of us and had already established a security command post on the injured *Cole* by the time we arrived. We immediately set up a five-hundred-meter perimeter incorporating both the pier and the surrounding water. We were also directed to set up a sniper team on the bridge of the ship itself to monitor the situation, glassing the entire perimeter constantly to ensure that no other bad actors got into the mix.

This was where Glen and I came in. We set up two teams to rotate on round-the-clock sniper watch, twelve hours on and twelve off. We had a .50-caliber sniper rifle and four LAW rockets on the bridge. Our task was to protect both the ship and the rest of the crew while repair and containment efforts were under way.

It was a tense situation. Our relationship with Yemen was not great. There was a powerful current of anti-American sentiment in the little country that included a history of kidnappings and sponsorship of terrorism. Standing there on the bridge of the crippled destroyer, we were acutely aware of all the nearby Yemeni weapons that were trained on us. It had the anxious, volatile feeling of a standoff. Our orders were simple: anything or anyone who breaches our perimeter, take them out.

Although no outright hostilities broke out, the perimeter was in fact tested a few times. Each time we saw a vessel encroaching on our perimeter we radioed the guys in the boats: "Hey, I've got someone coming in close at ten o'clock. It doesn't look serious, but they're on the fence."

Meanwhile, crews were furiously at work pumping bilge out of that gaping hole in the Cole's flank. It was a constant battle just to keep the vessel afloat, and for a while there it was touch and go. We nearly watched that destroyer sink.

The suicide bombers had rammed the ship right where the galley is located, and just at the time of day when a large number of sailors were lining up for lunch. The carnage was awful.

I talked with a few of the survivors to try to find out exactly what had happened, and how this absurdly low-tech assault had penetrated the Cole's security. The answer, in essence, was "Security? What security?"

When they described their security posture, I was appalled. Here we were, docked just off the coast of a hostile nation, and as protection they'd set up a few guys on the ship's rail with unloaded M14s. These soldiers had had no training on the M14. And I need to repeat one point: they were protecting a billion-dollar vessel by standing on its deck with weapons that were not loaded. Really?

I soon learned that, for all intents and purposes, this was standard security. Up until now, that is. After the Cole was hit, things changed fast. Soon the military was making it mandatory for at least

30 percent of every ship's crew to be actually trained in force protection.

When Glen took position on the bridge and I rotated off-watch, I went down a few floors to look around. I found a used coffee mug, washed it out, and brought it back up on deck to the temporary food station they'd set up at the back of the boat, where I used it to get a cup of hot coffee. I was just starting to get some of that hot java into me when I noticed one of the sailors staring at me.

"What?" I said.

He pointed wordlessly at my coffee mug. I turned it around and looked on its reverse side. I hadn't noticed, but the guy whose mug it was had written his name on it.

It was one of the guys who'd been blown up in the attack.

Maybe some would have been spooked and set that thing down in haste. For me it was just the opposite. This sailor had been one of the first to give his life in a war we didn't even know what to call yet. It was an honor to drink from that man's cup. I kept that mug and used it for the rest of our tour.

We were there on the *Cole* for about seven days. The ship was eventually boarded onto a huge Norwegian craft designed to carry offshore oil-drilling equipment and hauled back stateside, where after fourteen months of repair work it was returned to service.

CHAPTER THIRTY-NINE

After I got back from that deployment on the *Duluth*, two big changes were in store for me. I was about to become a father, and I would also soon be leaving GOLF platoon.

I was coming up for reenlistment again, which meant I had a cash bonus coming, something like $40,000. The problem was, reenlisting while stateside would mean I'd be heavily taxed, with a significant California tax on top of the federal bite. If I reenlisted in a tax-free combat zone, I would get the whole bonus. This would amount to a difference of something like fifteen grand. Fifteen grand can buy an awful lot of diapers.

It's not uncommon for command to send a guy overseas for a short deployment to help him out in circumstances like this. So I wound up joining ECHO platoon, the next platoon up for deployment.

I did not want to join ECHO. They had a terrible reputation. Everyone knew they were one big mess.

Ultimately, though, I decided to put my family first and agreed. It was a move I would soon regret.

I flew out to join the platoon on the aircraft carrier where they were doing the tail end of their workup, about a hundred miles off the coast of San Diego. When I got there, I met up with Chris Dye, who had just taken over as the platoon's new chief in the command's efforts to rehabilitate the outfit. Finding out that Chief Dye would be running things at ECHO cheered me up. Maybe this wouldn't be so bad.

He told me they were planning to do some fast-roping off a couple of helicopters the next day as part of a maritime ship-boarding op. They were short one castmaster and I was certified as one. The castmaster is in charge of rigging up the setup inside the helo, deploying the guys out on the rope, and making sure it all goes properly.

The next day, we got up in the air and started the exercise. I was watching the guys go out the door: one, two, three. Suddenly I saw an MP5 rifle falling from the sky.

I could not believe it. A SEAL team was fast-roping out of a helo—and some guy lost his weapon?

Nothing like that would ever have happened in GOLF platoon. If it had, the guy who did it would have been sent back to the fleet with his trident ripped from his chest. This was my introduction to the realities of ECHO platoon.

We had a 90/10 rule in the SEAL teams: 90 percent of the guys are going to be solid, and 10 percent will be guys you hope will get kicked out or transferred. The problem with ECHO platoon was that we had far more than our fair share of 10-percenters. It was so clear that they had never had any really good leadership. They'd had no one to look up to or learn from. Still, I felt like I had been yanked from playing on a World Series team and kicked downstairs to the farm league. I wanted to go back and beg for my old place on GOLF team again.

•   •   •

Over the weeks after I arrived, things gradually started looking better as a trickle of additional guys joined us after finishing whatever workup they were on, further helping shore up the platoon. Ali, our senior corpsman, and Chris were classmates of mine from BUD/S.

With Chris and Ali joining the platoon, it was feeling like a mini-reunion. I started feeling a bit better about my situation. Maybe life in ECHO platoon would be tolerable. I sure hoped so.

CHAPTER FORTY

ECHO platoon wrapped up the workout, and I was back home but about to rotate overseas with the platoon to the Persian Gulf. On September 11, 2001, I got up at the crack of dawn to go surfing. I knew it would be my last day to do this for a while, so I made the most of it.

When I got home, I found Gabriele sitting not five feet from the television, enormously pregnant, staring at the screen. It was early still, barely 6:00 A.M. on the West Coast. She turned to look at me, with an expression of speechless horror. I sat down next to her and we watched the second plane hit the South Tower of the World Trade Center in New York City.

Within days I had joined my platoon on a nonstop flight to the Middle East. Barely twenty-four hours after leaving San Diego we were receiving a briefing at Camp Doha, the principal U.S. base in Kuwait. We were told we would be participating in stopping Iraqi tankers in the gulf.

A year ago—even a month ago—I'd been looking

forward to exactly this mission. But now everything had changed. Our country had been attacked in a brutal and unprovoked strike that slaughtered thousands of civilians. It was payback time, and we were champing at the bit to get where we could do some serious damage in the name of our people back home. Stopping Saddam's oil smugglers, until recently a cherry assignment, now seemed like a time-consuming detour.

Still, this was a perfect mission for SEALs. We'd had teams supporting the operation for years, ever since Desert Storm in 1990.

These ships were coming out of Iraq sealed shut, tight as drums. To prevent being caught by boarding teams, these guys literally welded themselves in so nobody could get to them.

That was where we came in. We knew how to get on and into these boats silently, quickly, and effectively, in minutes. If the metal ship doors were welded shut, we would cut our way in through the roof with an acetylene torch. But we'd have to move fast, because the moment the smugglers realized they were being boarded they headed as quickly as possible for nearby Iranian waters—and if they made it, it was game over.

With the events of 9/11 just weeks behind us like a fresh and gaping wound, the air crackled with an angry electricity. Our platoon was outfitted in black from head to toe, wearing balaclavas, those ninja-style masks that conceal the entire head except the eyes. A few of our guys who spoke Arabic had dubbed our team *Shaytan abyath*, "the White Devils," after overhearing crews captured from a few of the smugglers' ships we'd taken down muttering the phrase in our direction. We embraced the name, and I used the idea of it in a patch I designed for our platoon: an image of a white devil on a black background underneath "3ECHO." In addition to our platoon patches, we also had NYFD patches sewn onto our uniforms to pay homage to fallen heroes back home.

The platoon left at sunset for its late-night operation on a small high-speed special ops boat called a Mark V. Once out in the middle of the international shipping lane, the platoon sat there silently in the dark, staging for minutes or hours, waiting for the word to go. Meanwhile, the platoon's sniper was nearby in the helo, quietly trolling the area and looking for targets.

As a sniper, you have the big picture in the helo. You orchestrate the silent, deadly nighttime dance. It's the sniper's job to identify targets using the helicopter's forward-looking infrared system (FLIR) and pass critical target information to the platoon. In the helo, we are the eyes of the operation. The FLIR, a glass bubble on the bottom of the craft, has a range of over fifty miles. Nestled in the back of the Sea Hawk, you sit there watching that eighteen-inch green screen with a clear view of what's happening miles away down on the gulf's surface. Once the team begins boarding the ship, you are the one passing real-time intel on all onboard activity to the team leaders. It's also your job to take out any targets that threaten the operation, if it comes to that, though this is a rare occurrence.

As Glen and I had done on the bridge of the crippled USS *Cole*, Chris and I shared this role. As sniper on duty, we'd participate in the nightly helicopter crew briefing, then hit the deck and take off in the bird to go cruising for targets. The rest of the platoon was stationed onshore at Camp Doha, and they would ride out every night in the Mark V, spend a few hours out on the gulf, and then, about 3:00 or 4:00 A.M., ride back in to Kuwait for the night. Not us. Because the helo deployed directly off the deck of the destroyer out in open waters, one of us would live all week on board the ship right along with the helicopter squadron. They set up a cot for us in the weapons hold area, where we would sleep with our guns. (We preferred to keep them on our person. What better way to know they were secure?) For all practical purposes, when not out on a mission we lived in that room.

We did this for weeks. Chris and I rotated out, trading off being on sniper watch and being part of the boarding teams. During the month or so we spent out there, we took down about half a dozen smuggling vessels.

CHAPTER FORTY-ONE

One day we got a briefing from National Security Agency (NSA) guys about a terrorist transport boat they'd been keeping an eye on. They thought it might be coming out of Iraq soon with a substantial cache of weapons and HVTs (high-value targets) on board. Whether "high-value targets" meant a known terrorist, hostile intel asset, or other person of interest, I didn't know, didn't need to know, and frankly didn't care. Whatever or whoever was on that boat, it was important. They described the target vessel's profile and gave us its identifying mark: Alpha-117.

This was the same ship, they said, that had been used by al Qaeda operatives to smuggle out the explosives that had been used to blow up U.S. embassies in Tanzania and Nairobi back in the summer of 1998. Those attacks had killed more than two hundred people, including a dozen Americans, and injured over four thousand more. That was the terrorist attack that had put Osama bin Laden on the map for the first time.

These guys were serious bad actors who had spilled American blood, and they would be armed. The intel guys were briefing all American assets in the region, they said, and then they gave us the rules of engagement for this particular situation. "If you guys see this target," they told us, "you're authorized to take it down." Period.

A few days passed, and Chris rotated out to the team while I took his place on sniper duty. As much fun as it was being part of the team in a smuggler takedown operation, I looked forward to being back on sniper watch. I have always loved flying, and this gave me the chance to go out every night in a bird. The nights when we didn't see any noncompliant vessels, the crew on the surface would have nothing at all to do, but even on those nights, up in the helo I was kept relatively busy manning the helo-based surveillance equipment, and I enjoyed it.

My first night back on watch, I sat in the back of an H-60 Sea Hawk helicopter as we made our way in slow, lazy arcs across the water and back.

I'd been staring at the FLIR screen for a while when I saw something that made me sit up straight. Right there on the pale green screen I could see the identifying numbers on the boat's stern: Alpha-117. I was staring at the target the NSA had briefed us on, the ship that had supplied the explosives that had taken out our embassies in Nairobi and Tanzania.

I radioed Lieutenant Chris Cassidy, our platoon commander on the Mark V. Word came back almost instantly. "Sniper One, this is ECHO One. We are taking her down. Get us good eyes on."

Now I briefed the helo crew. This was a much different situation than taking down a bunch of smugglers. They hadn't been in this type of situation before, and they were clearly nervous. We were going in to take down a hostile terrorist ship, and if those characters saw us coming they wouldn't be welding themselves in and waiting to see what we did. There were weapons on that boat for a reason. They'd use them on us.

I went back to Cassidy and started feeding him the information he needed to mount our silent attack. In this instant his concerns were pure physics and logistics. How do we get on board fast and clean? What class of ship is it? Where's the superstructure located—midship, foreship, aft? What's the ideal point on the ship to board? How long will it take the team to scale and board—how many feet of freeboard are we looking at?

In an operation like this, stealth and accuracy are everything. Unless you want to have the other guy's arsenal start unloading in your direction, you need to strike with the speed and accuracy of a snake. This is the quintessential sniper's task: instantaneous calculation, integration, and delivery of critical information, complete and with 100 percent accuracy.

I emptied my mind and focused my faculties like a laser sight. Right now I had to function as a precision instrument for surveillance and calculation. I started passing Cassidy the data he needed.

Cassidy spoke quietly into his comm, briefing the team. They hopped into two RHIBs (rigid-hulled inflatable boats). The RHIB is a very fast craft, with twin diesel engines delivering 1,000 horsepower. You come up alongside the ship, matching its speed, and pin your RHIB right up against the hull. This is a precision stunt, something like pulling up in a Hummer next to a bus going 60 mph on a highway and maintaining your position in perfect tandem while eight guys step over you and board the bus in full gear. One simple misstep can mess it up, and here that would have lethal consequences.

I had to be careful not to put the helo on scene too soon, because if the crew on the tanker was alerted by the sound of the approaching helo, we would lose the crucial element of surprise. I had to time it to the split second and coordinate the procedure precisely with the platoon on the water and pilots up front in the helo. Training, training.

In the waters off Iraq at midnight the assault sequence played out in a surreal silence, broken only by momentary brief murmurs into comms as critical bytes of information were passed on. From point man to breacher, every member of the team knew exactly what he had to do.

The operation went off like a precision electronic instrument. As the members of the assault team scrambled up narrow ladders and slipped silently over the rails, I sat up in the helo, peering out the open door, scanning the length of the terrorist boat, scrutinizing the scene through my night-vision goggles for the slightest trace of movement.

There was no one on deck. We had caught them completely off guard.

Without firing a shot, our guys took over the ship.

All told, we'd taken about thirty prisoners, a bunch of fake passports, over a hundred grand in U.S. dollars, and a lot of weapons. From start to finish, we pulled off this high-threat takedown in about five minutes, with maybe another ten to comb the ship and make sure everything and everyone was accounted for.

We would never know what happened or exactly what these characters were up to. But we did know that they were up to something big—and it wasn't good.

CHAPTER FORTY-TWO

On October 7, 2001, while my buddies and I were boarding oil smugglers off the coast of Iraq, President George W. Bush and Prime Minister Tony Blair each announced the commencement of Operation Enduring Freedom, a joint effort between the Afghan United Front and U.S. and U.K. forces to oust the Taliban and al Qaeda influence and destroy their terrorist training infrastructure in Afghanistan. That same day, American and British air forces began massive aerial bombardment of the capital, Kabul, and a few other key locations in Afghanistan.

Now we were headed there to join the action. We were briefed but we still didn't know exactly when or where we'd be going, or what we'd be doing when we got there. We *did* know that Afghanistan was home to a section of the Himalayan mountain range, and that we were not prepared for that kind of terrain. We were similarly unprepared for the weather. Temperatures could be up into the high nineties and higher during the day and then plummet to below freezing at night.

Soon the word came down: we were heading to Kandahar International Airport, one of the first bases we were establishing on the ground.

Kandahar airport would now become the base of operations for Task Force K-Bar, the spec ops group we would be joining. One of the first ground assault teams in the U.S.-led invasion, Task Force K-Bar was composed of special operations forces from eight different nations that were part of the Coalition fighting together: Australia, Canada, Denmark, Germany, New Zealand, Norway, Turkey, and the United States.

We were briefed, too, on the current rules of engagement (ROE). They were a surprise. The ROE seemed to boil down to this: you see any dark-skinned male of fighting age—that is, fifteen years old or older—and you're cleared to engage.

That was highly unusual. Normally the ROE for combat missions are pretty complicated and quite strict. We got the general impression that it was often difficult to know who was just a regular Afghan and who might be part of the Taliban or al Qaeda.

In the middle of December our boots hit Afghan soil for the first time. Rolling down the ramp of the C-130, hitting the ground and looking around, it felt like being dropped onto the set of a classic Vietnam movie like *Platoon* or *Apocalypse Now*. Helicopters filled the air; equipment was moving everywhere. Chaos.

That first week at Kandahar airport things were pretty crazy, as our command structure worked to set up a tactical ops center and hammer out some kind of order.

Kandahar airport also served as our prisoner-of-war staging camp. As the Afghanistan effort proceeded, all the Taliban, al Qaeda, and others who were captured in the field would be brought to the airport to be processed and interrogated before being flown to Guantánamo. By the time we got there, people had already set up a large prison camp facility that bore a striking resemblance to the POW camp I'd been incarcerated in at SERE school. It was surreal.

On Christmas Day 2001, we went out on our first patrol in Afghanistan. We spent all afternoon packing our gear and were ready for anything. We had the Mark 41 automatic grenade gun, which launches a series of mic-mic (40mm) grenades. It's like shooting a machine gun, only instead of bullets, you're firing a string of grenades. We had rocket launchers and LAW rockets strapped all over our vehicles, as well as a .50 cal and an M60 machine gun. Our comm antenna was hooked up so our comms guys could link into satellite, and we were all outfitted with night-vision gear. We were, in other words, loaded for bear.

The environment was not the sand desert of Kuwait but a rough, high desert terrain. We didn't encounter anyone during the patrol, but we kept seeing what we thought were land mines. We'd stop, our EOD (Explosive Ordnance Disposal) team would dismount and scope everything out, then they'd get back in the vehicle and we'd keep moving forward. Progress was slow and tense.

We also found discarded terrorist campsites in a cluster of trees, where Cassidy insisted we camp for the night.

The patrol was otherwise uneventful, and we headed back the following day, patrolling as we went. Although nothing much happened, it was good to shake out the cobwebs and get ourselves moving out there in the field.

CHAPTER FORTY-THREE

A few days after Christmas, an event occurred that showed us how little margin for error there was here.

About a thirty-minute drive from the Kandahar airport there was a place called Tarnak Farms, where the 9/11 attackers were said to have trained. The place had now been completely leveled by Coalition bombing raids, but it was still a useful training site. We had set up a mock shooting range there and would go out to test weapons, check our explosives, and blow off captured enemy ordnance.

Now, a few days before New Year's, we headed out there to do some more testing on our weapons and make sure our zero was good. Today I wouldn't need to go anywhere to confirm my rifle's zero. I could just plug my local coordinates into my software and it would correct for that part of the world, with its particular elevation, degree of latitude, and environmental conditions. Back in 2001 we didn't have that sophisticated software, and nothing could replace getting out on the range and physically testing the weapons. We also had a bunch of enemy ordnance we wanted to take out there to blow.

About half the platoon went out this time, maybe eight guys including our two EOD guys, and we took just two vehicles. We arrived and parked, and as I stepped out of the Humvee I happened to glance down at the rear tire. My eye caught a glimpse of something that looked like a pink pig's tail sticking out from under the tire. I bent down slowly to get a closer look.

It was det cord.

I froze. I'd done enough demolitions to know what I was looking at, but when you have an expert handy it never hurts to get a second opinion. So I called Brad, one of our EOD guys, over to take a look. This was a situation where it would certainly pay to be sure.

Brad stepped cautiously over and angled in close for a good look. "Okay," he said quietly, "everybody slowly step back."

Everybody slowly stepped back.

Brad called over the other EOD guy, Steve. Very slowly, very carefully, they checked the whole scene out, inch by inch.

"Okay, guys," Brad finally said, "here's the situation. We have parked directly on top of an antitank mine. Which happens to be tied into three antipersonnel mines."

It did not take a degree in physics or expertise in demolition specs to know that what our Humvee was sitting on was enough to blow us all to Pakistan.

We stood in place while Brad and Steve dismantled the whole mess, wondering how on earth we hadn't set the explosives off. I mean, we didn't just lightly brush the thing. We had parked a Humvee on it. Why were we still standing here, alive to tell the tale? Was the thing a dud, or were we just ridiculously lucky?

Our answer came soon enough. Brad came over to us after they'd finished their work and said, "Whoever set this thing up missed one step. They didn't set up the drum correctly. As a result, the pressure plate didn't rotate properly and it failed to initiate the charge. Which, all things considered, was a good thing."

We couldn't argue with that. Without that one human error, the thing would have gone off and taken all of us with it.

CHAPTER FORTY-FOUR

Shortly after New Year's Day we learned we would be going on a mission up north to the province of Khost, nestled in the mountains right up against the Afghanistan-Pakistan border. Khost is home to the Zhawar Kili cave complex, where Osama bin Laden is said to have officially declared war on America in 1998.

The second-largest known Taliban training camp in Afghanistan, Zhawar Kili was an elaborate complex of caves and tunnels built into the mountainside. This place was a key strategic flash point. It was one of the prime regions where al Qaeda and Taliban leadership were believed to have fled after we heavily bombed their cave hideouts at Tora Bora, some fifty miles to the north. It was also a major corridor to Pakistan.

Hard information on this cave complex was sketchy at best. We knew there was a base camp consisting of three large tunnels, with an unknown number of rooms, caves, and subtunnels. We also knew there was an extensive system of caves and tunnels built into the mountain ridge above the base camp. This place had arms depots, communications, hotel-like residences, a mosque, a kitchen, a medical facility, and more. It was an entire terrorist town drilled into the face of a mountain, with room for some five hundred people at a time.

The place was also a fortress. It had been hit by U.S. air strikes shortly after hostilities commenced on October 7, but to little effect. In order to really nail this place, we needed people on the ground exploring the caves themselves on foot and coming back with the specific coordinates that would allow precision strikes. That's where we came in.

Our air forces were going to launch a massive air strike, pounding the area with JDAMs (Joint Direct Attack Munition) to soften the target. Our SEAL platoon would go in the following day to bat cleanup.

Our platoon of sixteen was going to need some reinforcements, so our numbers were appropriately goosed with the addition of a ground unit of about twenty marines.

We also had our two air force CCTs (Combat Controllers), Brad and Eric, who always had air support at their fingertips the moment we needed it, and our two EOD guys, Brad and Steve. For this mission we were also assigned two guys from the FBI to provide forensic expertise and DNA-sample collection from enemy grave sites; one more from the Counterterrorist Intelligence Center (CTIC); and a chemical weapons expert from the army's Chemical Reconnaissance Detachment (CRD), all there for their expertise in combing through whatever we might find.

The plan was for the marines to insert with us, then split off and set up a defensive perimeter higher up on the ridge, making sure our backs were covered while we combed through the dozens of caves and tunnels doing BDA (bomb damage assessment) and documenting whatever was left behind. We would get into the valley, spend eight to ten hours on-site once we made our way to the cave complex, then extract and report back. It would be a solid one-day op, no vehicles, all on foot. Twelve hours from start to finish, max.

At least, that was the plan.

CHAPTER FORTY-FIVE

SUNDAY, JANUARY 6

It was about a three-hour insert by helicopter from Bagram Air Base to the Zhawar Kili complex. We were let off in the mountains well before dawn, about 4:00 A.M. We set up a quick perimeter, checked in with the marines (who had arrived a little ahead of us), made sure we were verified for where we were so our air support team would know we were friendlies and wouldn't take us out, and set up our rendezvous points for extraction at the end of the day. Then we set off, patrolling our way to the cave complex.

At the cave complex, we started at the base camp, taking it a cave at a time. Our planes had pounded the place. There had been quite a few people in there the night before, but now nothing was left except for bits and pieces of bodies, hardly anything even identifiable.

Inside the caves on the ridge it was a whole other story. These caves were so deeply burrowed into the mountain that many of them were still completely intact.

We started in, using a procedure similar to the way we would clear a house. Four of us would go in to clear a cave, then come out and report, then move on to the next, and the next, making sure each cave was clear as we went. One cave was an ammo bunker. The next was a classroom. Then there were living areas. It was an extensive network, with some of the tunnels interconnected, and it went on and on.

The caves were so deep that we couldn't see very far into them. Our night vision was severely limited, because you need at least a small bit of natural light to use it, and it was pitch black in there. We ended up inching through the caves using the paltry beams of illumination thrown by the small lights mounted on our weapons and clearing around corners with our good old-fashioned SureFire white-lens flashlights.

Those first few hours going deep into those caves and tunnels were intense. We had no idea what we'd find. We didn't know if we would run into anyone, or if there was possibly an ambush lying in wait for us, or if the caves were booby-trapped.

Fortunately we did not encounter a single person. There were, however, massive amounts of ordnance, ammo, and fuel, stacked floor to ceiling. They had stocked up on some big hardware, too, including tanks. These guys had prepared for quite the campaign.

We found classrooms with posters on the walls sporting anti-American slogans. On one the artist had cobbled together a photo of bin Laden in the foreground with two planes crashing into the Twin Towers in the background. I stared at this freakish piece of propaganda. This thing was created as an al Qaeda recruiting poster for the mission it illustrated. In other words, it had been put together *before* the event it was depicting had taken place. Standing there deep in the bowels of this mountain on the other side of the world, staring at a picture of the attack on New York City that was made and hung here before the attack itself actually occurred—it was one of the eeriest experiences I've ever had. I still have that poster.

It was hot, tedious, nerve-racking work. Within about four

hours we had the whole place cleared. Then we went back through the whole place a second time, gathering up intel, collecting the smaller items that we could bring back with us, and planting demolition in areas we would later blow. Brad and Eric recorded the exact GPS coordinates at the entrances to each cave so our guys could follow up with more accurate air strikes, since the shotgun approach of the night before had missed so much. The FBI guys had DNA kits as part of their mission, which was to ID whatever bodies we might find. As we worked, some of the others documented everything with video and tons of photographs.

After gathering everything we could take with us, we got it all ready to blow. We blew up the radios and a ton of ordnance. The explosion created a huge fireball that nearly consumed half the mountain. It was January 6, but it sure looked like the Fourth of July.

Daylight was starting to fade, and we got out of there and started the long hump back to the perimeter for our rendezvous. We were thirty minutes out from our scheduled exfil.

Nothing to do but sit and wait.

One of our EOD techs, Steve, started dumping his water. He'd been carrying extra bottles of water that they would use to shape blasting charges, and he figured now he wouldn't be needing any of it. That seemed crazy to me. That was drinkable spring water! When you're out in the field on any kind of recon, water is more precious than gold. He'd already dumped out several bottles when I saw what he was doing and stopped him.

"Hey, dude," I said, "give me the rest. I'll take all that."

Just then we heard the distant but unmistakable sound of the transport choppers, probably five to ten minutes away. They were coming to get us. But Captain Harward, back at TOC (tactical operations center) and on the radio with us, wanted us to go back and look for more DNA evidence. And, since we had already found a treasure trove of enemy resources that exceeded even the most optimistic expectations, that suggested there was even more out there.

In for a penny, in for a pound: now that we'd cracked open this prize, Harward wanted us to stay out there and see how much more we could dig up.

The sound of the helicopters briefly hovered, then slowly started to diminish. With our extraction just minutes away, Harward had turned them around. We were out there, on our own, for at least another day or two.

Steve looked at me in horror as I smacked my lips, having just polished off the last water bottle. He was devastated. What could I say? Hey, that's why you don't pour out your water, ever. You just never know what's going to happen.

So here we were, out in the middle of nowhere, deep in enemy territory, on our own for the night. We didn't have the proper clothing for the drop in temperature or equipment and supplies to set up a real camp.

We had passed an abandoned village at the top of a valley on our way to the caves. Chief Dye took four of us there to do a recon and clear it so we could occupy it.

It took us about an hour to get there. When we got close, it was pretty clear that the place had been completely deserted. Whoever had been there had probably left as soon as those bombs started falling the night before. Still, caution dictated that we assume nothing. We snuck around behind and approached from the rear. We cleared every room and made sure the place was secure. Then two of us went back to pass the word and lead everyone up there.

We figured we would use this place as a kind of forward operating base the whole time we were out there, however long that would turn out to be. It was a smart decision—because we would be out there in the wild for a lot longer than one or two days.

MONDAY, JANUARY 7

The next morning we split up. Part of the platoon went out with the forensics team to go dig up those grave sites and see if they could bring Harward some fresh, juicy DNA. Four of us—Cassidy, Chris, Brad, and I—went out before dawn to patrol a site where a C-130 gunship had engaged some forces the night before, to see if we could find any bodies.

We reached the coordinates we'd been given just moments before daybreak. Before we could do any serious searching, we heard voices coming from some nearby caves above us. The four of us instantly hit the ground and waited. As we watched, a spill of enemy fighters started pouring out of one of the caves—twenty, at least, and all armed.

We were outnumbered at least five to one, and we were not exactly armed with machine guns. These guys were headed our way. We would have to call in an air strike, and do it fast.

There was a B-52 nearby. Brad got it on the radio. It was my job to give him the coordinates. The only way to ensure that the team in the B-52 dropped their fireworks on the other guys and not on us was to give them exact coordinates. Typically we would do this using a high-powered laser rangefinder hooked into a GPS so that when it ranged the target it would give us not only distance but also the target's GPS coordinates, which we could then pass on up to whoever was on air support. These bombers are extremely accurate with their ordnance, like vertical snipers in the sky.

However, there was a snag.

We'd only planned for a simple twelve-hour mission and didn't have all our usual equipment. Typically, for a full-on recon mission, I'd have at least a good sniper rifle. We didn't have even a decent rangefinder.

Training, training. As a SEAL sniper I'd been taught to estimate distances on the fly even without all the usual tools, using only my five senses and my gut. But typically I'd be shooting a 10-gram bullet from the muzzle of a rifle. In this case, we were shooting a 1,000-pound "bullet" out of a 125-ton aircraft, flying twenty thousand feet above us at near the speed of sound, at a target less than five hundred yards away from where we sat—I had to get it right.

Range estimation. This was something else we covered in sniper school. You visualize a familiar distance, say, a football field. That's one football field, two football fields, three football fields . . . but this can be risky when you're not on level ground. Here I had to sight up a rugged, rocky incline. And daybreak lighting can play tricks with distances.

Those twenty-plus al Qaeda, or Taliban, or whoever they were, were trickling down the slope heading straight for our position. They hadn't seen us yet, but it would be only seconds before they did. If we were going to do this thing, it had to be now.

"Brandon!" Cassidy hissed. "You need to Kentucky-windage this drop!" "Kentucky windage" is a term that means basically this: Wing it. Give it your best shot. I gave Cassidy a bearing I estimated as 109 yards past the group. If I was going to be off at all, better to guess long than short. And if I was completely accurate, a drop a hundred meters behind them should at least buy us a few seconds to adjust and drop a second time.

Now the enemy cluster was so close we couldn't wait any longer. We were concealed but not covered. They couldn't easily see us, but once they knew where we were, our concealment would give no protection against incoming fire. We quickly moved to cover— and that's when they spotted us. There were a few alarmed shouts and then the sounds of small-arms fire.

There is nothing quite so galvanizing as the distinct crack! snap! of semiautomatic weaponry being fired over your head, the crack! being the sound of the initial shot itself and the snap! being the bullet breaking the sound barrier as it zings past you.

We returned fire. I sighted one guy wearing a black headdress and dropped him. I quickly resighted and dropped a second guy, this one wearing the traditional Afghan wool roll-up hat. Then I sighted a third. I glanced up and saw vapor trails in the sky. The B-52 was flying so high it was invisible to us, but I knew exactly what was happening up there. They were dropping the first bomb.

When you are this close to a big explosion it rocks your chest cavity. You want to make sure your mouth is open so the contained impact doesn't burst your lungs. Brad got the call. We were seconds from impact. We opened our mouths, dropped, and rolled.

The JDAM is a big bomb and extremely accurate. When the first set of JDAMs hit, it shook the mountain under our feet, throwing rubble everywhere.

I whipped around and glanced back up the incline to assess the strike. Perfect—about a hundred yards behind the target. I rolled again, adjusting numbers in my head, and quickly shouted the new coordinates to Cassidy, who gave them to Brad to relay up to the bird. In moments like this your senses go into hyper-acute mode and seconds seem to stretch into minutes, hours, a timeless series of discrete snapshots. I focused on my breathing, making it slow and deliberate, feeling the cool morning air mixed with the distinct smell of explosives teasing my lungs. I knew my numbers were accurate and that the men shooting to kill us would themselves be dead in seconds. For a brief moment, I was at peace. And then an unexpected sound sliced through the strange silence: the wail of a baby crying.

My stomach twisted. I had a five-week-old baby boy, Jackson, at home whom I'd not yet held in my arms. Hopefully, I would survive this war to meet him face-to-face. Someone up on that hillside had a baby they would never see or hold again.

I knew these people had made the decision to bring their families out here, that they knowingly put them in harm's way. Sometimes, I'd heard, they even did this intentionally, using their own children, their flesh and blood, as living shields to prevent us from attacking. It was their choice, I told myself, not ours. But I'll never forget the sound of that baby's cry.

We opened our mouths, ducked, and rolled.

The second drop took them all.

CHAPTER FORTY-SIX

TUESDAY, JANUARY 8

Two big H-53 helos landed with a resupply we'd called in the night before. They had brought a few large cases of radio batteries—enough to last a month of talking twenty-four hours a day. Then they kicked out just one case of water and one case of MREs and took off.

This was likely a classic case of military miscommunication. Someone had probably passed on our request without specifying exactly how much food and water we would really need.

While patrolling the area we wound up capturing three guys in a little white Datsun pickup. They spoke Pashtun, and with the help of an interpreter we found out they came from a village we thought we had cleared. We went back and found a huge cache of weapons that we made sure were destroyed.

• • •

Now, in addition to keeping ourselves alive, we had three prisoners to keep, feed, and guard in our little village.

WEDNESDAY, JANUARY 9

We went out on patrol again and found another village to clear, this one fairly substantial in size. We divided up the platoon, each of us clearing half the village to make sure it was abandoned. It was, and we collected a good amount of both weapons and intelligence, including all sorts of plans and notes.

As we were doing this, we had one of the biggest—and certainly happiest—surprises of our entire deployment. From inside the village we had just cleared, who should come trotting out toward us but a small, light tan puppy. Last thing we expected to see, that was for sure. We named him JDAM, and he became our platoon mascot.

THURSDAY, JANUARY 10

We set up a reconnaissance position so we could have the whole valley in view and watch enemy forces sneak back and forth along a series of mountain trails that led across the border into Pakistan.

By now we knew there was a significant level of enemy activity going on in the valley. The idea was for two teams to hide out for the entire day and fill in as many details as possible.

Once we reached the ideal elevation and found an appropriate hide site, we called the marines who were on their way to meet us. It turns out they had stumbled across a cluster of heavily armed Afghans, who dropped most of their guns and ran. They left behind guns, rocket launchers, grenades, a whole armory.

The Afghans had been set up not 150 yards from a road they'd probably seen us traveling before. They were clearly waiting to ambush us. They knew we were operating in this area and figured one of our daytime patrols would pass by again sooner or later.

We figured out that our truck must have woken them around 3:00 A.M. They shook off their sleep and were in the process of setting up for the day when the marines, traveling on foot, stumbled into them.

We spent the day out there, but we saw little, and did not get much to bring back in the way of intel.

FRIDAY, JANUARY 11

We went out on another village op. There was a place we'd been watching for a few days. The people appeared to be farmers, but we were not 100 percent positive. We decided to go out there and see up close. I was set up as sniper overwatch to guard the platoon as they went in.

I watched as Cassidy and his team made their way up to where a small group of these guys were congregated in a few buildings. I used the scope on my .300 Win Mag sniper rifle to get a closer look at these people. I caught a glimpse of a few of them running around, as if they were in a rush to get something done. Something felt suspicious about it to me, but it could also be completely innocent.

I relayed my observations to Cassidy on the radio and told him to be on his toes.

As I continued shifting my view back and forth between Cassidy and his team and the little knot of Afghan farmers, I noticed one guy standing off to the side. He had a gun.

The man had his rifle slung casually over his shoulder, and there was nothing threatening about the posture. I couldn't tell if he was a bad actor or an innocent farmer. I was leaning toward farmer—but why was he carrying a gun? Alarm bells started going off in my head.

The guy was about six hundred yards away, slightly more than six football fields. I knew I could take him out in a heartbeat. No problem. I felt my finger against the trigger.

But if I did, it would certainly complicate the situation. If I shot the guy and it turned out he was innocent, we'd have quite a scene on our hands. On the other hand, if I didn't and he wasn't innocent, the team could be in danger.

I had all the information I was going to have. It came down to pure instinct. Do I take the shot, or not?

I breathed out . . . focused . . . squeezed . . . I decided not to take the shot.

A moment later Cassidy and the guys were there, talking to these Afghan farmers—and suddenly I caught a glimpse of movement way off to my left. Some character in Arab dress, clearly not Afghan, was hightailing it out of there, tearing along a little goat trail up the mountain toward Pakistan for all he was worth.

They'd been hiding him. That's what I'd been sensing. The Afghan farmer I'd been targeting had been standing sentry, trying very hard not to look like that was what he was doing. They were covering for this al Qaeda dude or whoever he was, and the moment they had Cassidy and his team engaged in conversation, one of them had told him to take off.

I switched to my binos and caught him scurrying up the mountain, closing in on him a kilometer away. I couldn't get an accurate shot off in time, and I couldn't go after him, because to do that I'd have to leave my hiding spot and would no longer be supporting Cassidy and the team. I didn't have the radio resources to call in close air support, and in moments he would be over the border.

I got back to Cassidy on the radio and told him what had happened. I could see him now, going back and forth with the farmers, who were hotly denying everything. I'd seen enough to know they were lying.

Thinking back over the whole sequence, I didn't see what I would have done differently. With the information I had, giving this farmer the benefit of the doubt still seemed to me the right decision. Yes, these Afghan village people would sometimes harbor other Afghans who were Taliban or Arabs we would call al Qaeda. For the most part, though, they were not bad people; they were just trying to get along and survive, to go on living there in the mountains the way they had been for generations, without getting caught in the crosshairs of battle.

CHAPTER FORTY-SEVEN

SATURDAY, JANUARY 12

We had now been holed up in this mountain range for a week and had cleared out a ton of enemy resources, taken a handful of prisoners, and racked up dozens of enemy KIA (killed in action), but there were still a lot of bad actors in the area that we hadn't been able to track down.

Chris and I wanted to get out there on our own, just the two of us, and patrol the area without having to be tied to a whole squad. Cassidy and Chief Dye gave us the thumbs-up.

When we got into position we saw one Afghan and followed him. On this day, it was not our marksmanship we'd be practicing but our stalking craft. As much time, energy, training, and focus as we put into our marksmanship skills, the core skill of the expert sniper is not to shoot. It is to hunt. If intellectual capacity is a sniper's foremost qualification, the number two trait is patience. We will take out any enemy we have to when the situation calls for it, whether that means using a rifle, a handgun, a knife, or our bare hands. Yet the sniper's fundamental craft is not killing a person, but being able to get close enough to do so. Chris and I were on a classic sniper stalking mission: track, sneak up, observe, and disappear again, leaving no trace behind.

The man was moving out now, ready to start his day. So were we.

A short while later we found the spot the man and a few of his cohorts had been using to lay up at night. There was a bedroll stash, food and water, some ammo, and evidence of a small fire for cooking. Chances were very good they'd be back that night. We marked the GPS coordinates and backed out again, leaving everything exactly as we found it, and moved on.

We spent the day out there, covered a good ten to twelve kilometers and located about half a dozen sites.

We got back to camp about midnight. After reporting in, we sat down and put our notes together, lining up all the coordinates so we had a tight sequence.

The site we had occupied with Chief Dye that first night at Zhawar Kili gave us an amazingly clear view of the valley below, such that we were able to gaze out with our binos and get an easy visual on all the locations we'd marked during the day. We saw the barest flicker here, a glint there, telltale flashes as the men fired up their cook stoves and campfires signaling us that, yes, the sites were occupied again.

By this time we were already familiar with the process of calling coordinates in ourselves. So, that's what Chris and I did. We had laid this gigantic trap. And we got to be the ones to spring it.

Boom! Boom! Boom!

One direct hit followed another. It was done.

SUNDAY, JANUARY 13

We choreographed one last hurrah. All the intel we'd gathered over the week was orchestrated into one final bombing session, the largest since the bombing of nearby Tora Bora exactly one month earlier. We pounded that place, and caved in the side of the mountain.

Our twelve-hour mission had turned into a military and political bonanza. In a network of more than seventy caves and tunnels, we'd uncovered nearly a million pounds of ammunition and equipment, along with a ton of intelligence, including extensive papers documenting cross-border traffic and other aspects of enemy tactical plans. More than 400,000 pounds of ordnance was dropped on the targets we flagged. We had destroyed one of the largest terrorist/military training facilities in the country and had taken out a significant number of enemy personnel.

MONDAY, JANUARY 14

On the ninth day of our twelve-hour mission, we boarded a pair of helos and lifted out of Zhawar Kili, bound for Bagram and Kandahar.

PART SIX
CONTINUING TO PROTECT AND DEFEND

CHAPTER FORTY-EIGHT

A few months later, I left Afghanistan with my platoon. I flew a third of the way around the world, grabbed a ride to my home in Point Loma, California, and met my son Jackson for the first time.

Jackson was now five months old. He had been born one month after I left the States. Coming face-to-face with him for the first time was incredible. I don't know what was more amazing to me: the fact that this little redheaded creature with ten fingers and ten toes was our son, or the fact that I'd made it back from Afghanistan to see him with all my ten fingers and ten toes intact.

When you get home from a six-month deployment you get sixty days' leave to decompress. I spent pretty much all of it with Gabriele and Jackson. It was a blast. Two solid months went by as if it were a single day.

On my way back to the States I had learned that I was leaving the SEAL teams. I'd been given orders to a newly formed Naval Special Warfare Group One Training Detachment (TRADET).

Change was afoot. With the growing importance of special operations in the warfare of the twenty-first century, the SEALs were undergoing reorganization. Prior to this, each individual SEAL team was responsible for its own training. Now all the advanced training was being put together under two divisions, one for each coast. TRADET was in charge of developing programs of advanced training, a sort of "continuing education" for SEALs beyond BUD/S and the other basic training courses. It was split up into different areas of training, including MAROPS (maritime operations), Land Warfare, Assault, and a handful of others.

Since TRADET was brand new, they badly needed warm bodies, especially bodies with experience. Sometimes there was a bit of arm-wrestling in terms of which group got which talent coming in fresh from the field, a little like the competition that happens when top players are drafted onto pro football teams.

When I checked out of SEAL Team Three and into TRADET one sunny day in early June, I was first placed in the Land Warfare office, but that posting didn't stick. Within a few days a request came from another division that set the course of my career for the next several years. The guys running the sniper division said they wanted me. So I was out of Land Warfare and into a tiny unit called Sniper Cell.

I felt incredibly fortunate to be recruited into Sniper Cell. For one thing, the group was so small it felt like my contribution could actually make a difference. It varied as people rotated in and out, but five members was typical. Most of the TRADET training groups were two to three times that size. Also, only the West Coast had a dedicated entity focused on advanced sniper training. Our Sniper Cell was the only one.

Another reason I felt so fortunate was that Sniper Cell was run by Chief Gardner, a veteran SEAL. Chief Gardner has an amazing résumé of service. He is the nicest guy you'll ever meet, but you do not want to go up against him in combat. The man is a killing machine. He was also a fantastic boss.

Since TRADET was new, we had to come up with new standardized training practices and programs for the cell. Because of my SAR background and real-world experience as a helo sniper, Chief Gardner put me in charge of developing a curriculum for the Helo Support block. A separate training for Helo Support was a brand-new concept, and for the most part the curriculum had to be created from scratch. And it had to be done fast.

Fortunately, I had an excellent ally in this project: Eric Davis, an old friend I'd known since BUD/S. Eric is a superstar instructor, one of the best I've ever seen. I would sit in on one of Eric's classes and get so engaged listening to him teach that I'd blink and an hour had gone by. And he wasn't just a good lecturer. He also genuinely cared about the students. I couldn't have wished for a better partner in the work we were about to undertake.

Chief Gardner gave us free rein to put together whatever we thought made the most sense for the new Helo Support block, and we threw ourselves into the task. I talked to every sniper I could find with significant helicopter experience to get their input and make sure I had the latest crew communication language. Then I wrote, wrote, and wrote some more. I was responsible for coordinating airspace, air assets (always challenging), live-fire ranges, boats, air flow out to San Clemente Island (where the bulk of our training was conducted), and the actual training of the platoon snipers. It was an insane flurry of activity, and it felt a little like jumping out of a plane at twenty thousand feet—exhilarating and terrifying.

CHAPTER FORTY-NINE

Everyone had always complained that helicopter assets were next to impossible to come by for training purposes. I was determined that this was not going to be a problem for our course. I had strong relationships in the helicopter community. I figured I could get us live resources, which from my perspective were essential. Simulators are fine, as far as they go, but anytime you can get your guys into a real helicopter, show them how to rig up their weapons in the door, give them live-fire training at some real target on the ocean's surface, both during the day and also at night with night-vision gear and lasers, you're going to have really superior results. When Air Operations scheduling reported that there were no assets available for us, I made it happen anyway. I refused to compromise. Sometimes we'd have helo assets come pick us up and fly us out to San Clemente Island, and sometimes we'd take our guys on a quick plane ride and meet the assets wherever they were. Whatever it took.

Something else that had always bugged me about Helo Support operations was the lack of a clearly integrated, efficient communications protocol. With a handful of different procedural standards being thrown together into the mix of an op, sometimes it was almost like trying to work in metric and inches at the same time. That had to change. I developed a new system of standardized operations and communications procedures between pilots and snipers. In terms of long-term impact, I believe this was my biggest accomplishment while running the Helo Support block.

We were inventing everything on the fly (literally!), but I loved the challenge. In about a month I had a complete curriculum developed and ready to teach. Now all I had to do was start teaching it, something I'd never done before.

I remembered my own sniper training and how there were some instructors who really didn't know how to teach. I was determined not to be one of those. So I went to Instructor Training School. I can't say enough good things about it. All the public speaking and teaching I've done since has been tremendously influenced by my experiences at that school. They put us up in front of a classroom and videotaped us while we taught. Then they played the tapes back to us. There is nothing like watching yourself teach on videotape. We sat there staring at ourselves on screen and heard ourselves say "Uh" and "Um" and "Y'know" ten, twelve, fifteen times a minute. It was brutal. If you have any intention of teaching or being in any kind of leadership position, I highly recommend you do this.

Guys watched in horror as they saw themselves cursing in the middle of their sentences, saying things they would have sworn they never said until they saw the hard evidence. Talk about shock and awe. It was embarrassing—or it would have been if the instructors had rubbed our noses in it. But they had a job to do, and they got on with it. They would count up all the uhs, ums, and whatevers, all the curse words, then make us do it again. They drummed all the verbal tics out of us.

They taught us how to work off a curriculum, how to structure a class, how to gauge how each student was doing and how to support slower ones without browbeating them. They taught us it was okay to pause and gather our thoughts without filling in the empty space with an "Um." We learned how to ask questions without drilling students to the point where we'd make them uncomfortable. We learned how to encourage students to ask their own questions. And we learned how to get them thinking so they really absorbed the material instead of just parroting it back. They taught us how to teach. In terms of practical life skills, it was one of the best schools I've ever attended.

CHAPTER FIFTY

Once Eric and I had the Helo Support block up and running, Chief Gardner asked me to assist him with the redesign of Urban Sniper Training, which he had been putting together based in part on his experiences in Somalia. We did this right in San Diego in some old buildings that were owned by the Naval Training Center. Urban is all about trying to cover as many angles as you can and using cover effectively as you move through a village or city. We took our guys through our urban scenarios as two-man units, showing them how to set up urban hides—instead of going up on the rooftops where everyone expects you to be, find a basement where you can get eyes on your target. We also taught them how to disguise their hideout sites so they could shoot out of them with a clear line of sight, but no one could see into them.

We ran another block called Rural Training, where we brought guys who'd been through all the other training out hunting whitetail deer and elk. Hunting deer is typically much harder than hunting people. People get lazy. Wild animals do not. Their instincts are honed to a razor's edge. Taking our snipers out into the wild, having them stalk a live animal, get it on target, and stop a beating heart—it was phenomenal training, and one of my favorite parts of everything we did.

We would hunt in the mornings, hold long-distance shooting classes in the afternoon, and then hunt again in the evening. Our students blew the minds of some local hunters, because we were nailing deer at pretty long distances, from six hundred to eight hundred yards.

Every year, at the end of the year, they would traditionally give one person in the entire command a meritorious promotion. I knew very well that in this command I was surrounded by superstars. Chief Gardner had put me in, though, and to my great surprise, at the end of 2002, after six months at Sniper Cell, I was selected for early advancement and meritoriously promoted to petty officer first class, E-6. It was one of the proudest moments of my navy career.

CHAPTER FIFTY-ONE

In the summer of 2003, after I'd been at TRADET for a little over a year, Chief Gardner came to Eric and me one day and told us that the guys who ran the basic SEAL sniper school had come to him for some help.

"They're completely redoing the course," he said, "and they need a few experienced guys to go through a pilot version with them and decide which parts of the curriculum to lock down. I thought we could loan you two out for a few months."

Eric and I both felt honored to be asked. Rewrite the basic sniper school course, from the ground up? Talk about having an impact on the future of the U.S. military!

It reminded me of an amazing experience I'd had the year before, soon after I arrived at Sniper Cell. I'd been selected by WARCOM, the parent command for all the SEAL teams, to represent the entire SEAL community at Spec Ops Command in a review-and-selection process for the new SOPMOD (Special Operations Peculiar Weapons Modification) kit's weapon upgrade. The

SOPMOD kit consists of everything that goes with our basic assault rifle, the M4, including flashlight, laser (visible and infrared), hand grips, scope, night sight, etc.

I sat on a board with my corresponding representatives from the army and the air force, reviewed vendors' presentations, tested out all sorts of weapons and other equipment, and determined what equipment the next special ops generation would be using. It had been a huge responsibility—and an incredible honor.

It's rewarding to be part of a team where you're valued for your experience and where you're able to genuinely influence change. That was the atmosphere Eric and I encountered out at Camp Atterbury, where we spent three months working hard on developing the new curriculum. We all worked like crazy to nail down that pilot course, redesigning things on the fly just as we had with the elements of the advanced courses at TRADET. It was an all-out ninety-day sprint.

When the pilot course was finished, we returned to our posts at TRADET, where we resumed teaching our training blocks, and life went back to normal—but not for long. Shortly after we got back from that stint, Chief Gardner came to talk to Eric and me again.

"Senior Chief Nielson wants you down at the sniper school full-time to continue reworking the course," he said. Apparently, Senior Chief Nielson had been selling this idea hard to our command. It had taken some doing, because both Eric and I were only halfway through a three-year commitment to TRADET. Yet he managed to swing it.

Thus began another intense period of redesign. But this time we were shaping the entire basic core training of all future SEAL snipers—shooting, stalking, the whole thing.

It was an incredibly creative time. We would roundtable our ideas, make decisions, and implement them the next day. We started going over everything we'd experienced when we had gone through the course ourselves. We addressed whatever weak spots we'd seen. Before long we were completely overhauling the course, updating all the existing classes and adding some new ones.

For example, we began aggressively integrating technology into the training. At the time, sniper students were still being taught to survey their target terrain with binos and to then sketch it out by hand. We started showing our guys how to shoot and crop digital photos with Nikon cameras. We taught them how to use DLT-3500 software (the military version of Photoshop) to adjust levels and enhance a photograph's readability and clarity, and how to record their field intelligence on a laptop, compress and encrypt the data, and send it via satellite back to the base. This turned into a mandatory two-week program called PIC (photographic intelligence course) that new students had to take just before starting regular scout/sniper school.

We introduced ballistic software programs and focused on making sure these guys had a thorough understanding of external ballistics. In the old course we were basically taught to call the wind and shoot well, period. Now we started digging into the subject and turning these guys into ballistics experts.

We used technology to get more exacting with our weapons as well. When I entered the course back in 2000, I had been stuck with a faulty sight that could have gotten me washed out if I hadn't insisted on having the rifle tested. Too often, I had seen similar problems tripping up great shooters. Now we had the technology to solve these problems before they happened. We taught our students how to use a chronograph, a device that measures the muzzle speed in fps (feet per second) for each specific rifle.

Let's say you have two identical .300 Win Mag bolt-action rifles, both from the same manufacturer and even from the same manufacture batch. One could still be as much as several hundred fps slower than the other. For that matter, there are even differences in individual lots of ammunition. Granted, these differences will typically affect accuracy only to a minute degree. But, add them all together, especially when you're shooting at very long ranges, and the differences can have a critical impact. Perhaps we will eventually reach a level of manufacturing precision where that difference decreases to the point of insignificance. Perhaps. Right now, though, these individual differences are a fact of life, and we decided it was time to deal with it.

A chronograph can also help gauge the condition of the barrel. As I mentioned before, these rifles have a certain barrel life. Put your .300 Win Mag through a few thousand rounds and the barrel will start to go, which means your bullets will become inaccurate. We shot each student's rifle through a chronograph to find out quickly whether or not its barrel had gone beyond its useful life.

Eric transformed the KIM class by pioneering a whole new way of teaching memorization skills. Rather than relying on pure rote memory, with its endless repetition, he employed some impressive techniques that involved linking the objects or numbers you wanted to memorize with a systematic sequence of objects or sounds in your mind.

Eric was a master at this. Just before teaching his first class of a new KIM session, he would look at the student roster and in five or ten minutes code all their data and store it into his memory. Then he'd walk into class, look at the assembled students, point to one at random and say, "Okay, you over there, what's your name?" The guy would tell him his name, and Eric would nod and say, "Right, your Social Security number is . . ." and rattle off the guy's social and phone number. Then he'd do the same thing with everyone else in the room. I watched him do this over and over, and it never failed to blow the minds of everyone in the class. Mind you, Eric didn't have any natural gift of photographic memory. This was trained memory, and he trained all our guys to have that ability too.

For my part, I pushed hard on shifting the curriculum so that all our students would come out of the course knowing how to deploy independently, as solo operators. The way it was before, you'd have one student who happened to be a little better on the spotting scope, while his partner might be a little weak on ballistics but be a crack shot. To me, that was a recipe for breeding weakness into our graduates. It seemed to me we needed to make sure that every one of these guys we graduated had a complete command of every piece of the picture and could deploy by himself. Practically speaking, in most of the jobs they would be doing out in the field they would be called upon to act as lone gunmen.

Now we were graduating guys who were going out into the field and being absolutely deadly, whether in pairs or on their own.

CHAPTER FIFTY-TWO

Our instructors were teaching better, and our students were learning better. The course standards got harder, but instead of flunking higher numbers of students, we started graduating more. Before we redid the course, SEAL sniper school had an average attrition rate of about 30 percent. By the time we had gone through the bulk of our overhaul, it had plummeted to less than 5 percent.

For the first few pilot courses, we had constantly changed things around and experimented, designing and implementing improvements and refinements on the fly. By the end of 2004, after we'd been doing this for about a year straight, we settled on a finalized curriculum that we then continued to teach without much change—but we also built into it the idea of continuous improvement. So now the course goes through an annual review to make sure it continues to adapt to changes on the battlefield and to new developments in technology.

• • •

Earlier I said that intellectual or mental strength is the most important trait in a sniper, and that physical ability, as important as it is, is only 10 percent of the game. Of all the changes we made in the sniper course, the one that felt most significant to me and that I was proudest of was our system for mental management.

When we first encountered the concept of mental management it was being taught exclusively to instructors as a way to help us coach and teach more effectively. In essence, it was all about where we as instructors focused a student's attention.

Say you're doing batting practice with a kid and you notice he's standing with his knees buckled in, shoulders misaligned, hands spread wide apart on the bat. Your impulse might be to start telling the kid everything he's doing wrong. If you focus his attention on all these wrong things, though, what you're really doing is imprinting them into the poor kid's mind, with the result that they start becoming ingrained habits. If you say, "Hey, you're flinching. Every time the ball comes at you, you're flinching!" then what is that little kid thinking about? He's thinking about flinching—what he should not be doing.

If, instead, you say, "Put your hands closer together, and stand with your feet apart," then you're helping him focus on what he *should* be doing.

A beginner typically starts out very focused on everything that's going on. He'll tend to absorb whatever is thrown at him. So, as an instructor, are you going to feed him bad habits or good habits?

This all translated directly to instruction on the sniper course. In the old days instructors barked at us for everything we did wrong. We learned we could give a student three positive commands, three things he could do to correct errors, to help him develop good habits from day one.

We hired Lanny Bassham, an Olympic Gold Medal sports shooter and one of the pioneers of mental management to help us apply his methods to our sniper course—for the instructors and for the students, too. We also studied what the British and the army and marines were doing and consulted with coaches of a wide range of champion athletes. We ran a few pilot courses, experimenting in our live laboratory, trying out different techniques and seeing how each one affected the students. Eventually, we developed an entire system of mental management and integrated it into our marksman-ship class.

The first time I started teaching the mental management mate-rial as part of our course, some of the students were skeptical (and I admit that I had been too, at first). We issued Lanny's book to the whole class, but two guys also listened to Lanny's CDs every night. When the class's first shooting test came up, these two guys both shot perfect 100s. We had never had a pair shoot perfect 100s. In the second part of the test, they shot 100 and 95. It was the highest score in U.S. Navy SEAL sniper course history. Suddenly all the skeptical guys were begging to borrow the CDs and burn copies for themselves.

CHAPTER FIFTY-THREE

Barely a month after Eric and I had checked into WAR-COM, Senior Chief Nielson pulled me into his office to tell me he was retiring and that Master Chief Harvey Clayton was replacing him. I barely knew Clayton, just enough to say hi as we passed in the halls. I knew he had run the course many years earlier. I also knew he'd spent most of his time in the fleet navy and had really absorbed that culture—not usually a good mix with SEALs. What's more, while he was a very good match shooter, Harvey had never done any kind of operational tour.

Also, Clayton had a reputation—and it wasn't good.

Senior Chief Nielson shook his head, understanding the upset look on my face. He did, though, have something else to tell me. He was setting me up to be the sniper course manager.

This was no small thing. To put it in perspective: typically, E-5 and E-6 petty officers were sniper school instructors. They reported to the course manager, usually a chief petty officer, who managed the curriculum and ran the whole course. The course manager, in turn, reported to the division officer, currently Senior Chief Nielson, but soon to be Master Chief Harvey Clayton. The division officer ran interference between the course itself and the parent command. I was still an E-6, and teaching this course was my first LPO (leading petty officer) billet. By making me course manager, Senior Chief Nielson was saying he would be giving me an E-7 billet—in essence, setting me up to make chief petty officer the moment I became eligible.

Advancement to chief petty officer (E-7 and above) is a big deal in the navy. It's more than just a pay raise. Chief petty officers are considered a breed apart, a community within the community. And making chief after being in just over ten years? That would be a seriously big deal. A lot of guys go their whole careers without making chief.

I understood what Senior Chief Nielson was saying and what it meant—but, man oh man, I did not want to work for Clayton.

As it turned out, working for Harvey Clayton was not as bad as I'd expected. It was worse. Of all the leaders good and bad, all the bosses I've had throughout my entire career, Master Chief Harvey Clayton was the worst.

Harvey was not into technology, progress, or change. He was not interested in whatever improvements and new developments we wanted to bring to the course. If he had supported us the way Senior Chief Nielson had, or even just stayed out of the way and let us do what we were there to do, he could have taken credit for all of it and we would have been happy to let him do it. He couldn't get his own ego out of the way long enough to see that. Instead, he just wanted to rewind everything and have it all go back to the way it used to be. He also was quite clear that he was in charge. It was his show, and if he said no, that meant no.

Among other things, he contradicted instructors in front of the students. That's one of the last things you want to do. If one of your instructors does mess up, you pull him aside afterward and talk to him in private. Clayton's behavior was undermining the whole concept of respect for leadership. Neither the instructors nor the students could stand him.

Soon everyone was coming to me, complaining about the latest thing Harvey had done. It was a nightmare, but I didn't know what any of us could do about it. I started worrying that the course's reputation would suffer. If that started happening, it could unravel everything we were working so hard to accomplish.

Toward the end of 2004, I was about to start teaching a new course in the way we had agreed upon in a staff meeting. I had spent some hours prepping the course, redoing it and getting all the materials together so I'd be ready to go. Then, literally about an hour before the class was scheduled to start, Chris, one of our chiefs, came to tell me that Clayton wanted me to teach it the way it had been done before.

I lost it. This was my course. A few minutes later Clayton showed up, and I reamed him out, right in front of the other instructors.

"I'll tell you what, Harvey," I said. "If we were on a pirate ship at sea right now, I would shoot you in the back, toss you over the side, and declare mutiny."

I know, I know. This is not the recommended manner for addressing one's superior officer. I value respect as much as any SEAL, and I don't lose my cool very often. This was one of those rare moments, and master chief or no, I let him have it.

Clayton backed down, and I taught the course the way we had all agreed on before.

I knew this was the beginning of the end, though. For close to a year I'd done my best to be loyal to the guy and work things out, and the situation had gone from bad to worse. For everyone, morale hit a new low.

At the time, we had three instructors who were newly minted chiefs. They were with us while waiting to ship out to leadership posts. They all outranked me, so I went to them and asked for their help with Clayton.

Understandably, they were extremely reluctant to take any action. In the military, there is hardly anything you can do to ruin your reputation worse than going up the chain of command to complain about a superior. Whether you're talking army, air force, marines, or navy, I don't care what division or what force, ratting on your superior officer is putting your professional life and your reputation on the line. In a situation like this, it's far easier and safer to take the path of least resistance. Wait it out. Grin and bear it. But we'd been doing that for close to a year.

Of the three, Chief Chris finally went to our command's master chief and complained about Clayton. I don't know exactly how he did it, and I don't know exactly what he said, but whatever he did, it didn't work. Nothing happened to Clayton. But Chief Chris got demoted. He went from the number two spot to the last in line, and they pulled him from the course. You don't recover from something like that. From that point on, Chris had no hope of ever making master chief. It was a career-destroying move.

Not surprisingly, the two remaining chiefs weren't going to make any moves against Clayton. Not ever.

So it was up to me.

CHAPTER FIFTY-FOUR

I knew it could be the end of my career in the navy, but we couldn't keep operating like this. Clayton was messing up the course. You go out into the jungle and mess with a lion cub, you will hear about it from the lioness. The sniper course was my cub, and as long as there was breath in my body I was not going to let anyone compromise the integrity of what we had all worked so hard to build. Not even if it meant my career.

I started carefully documenting all of Clayton's bad behavior. I didn't editorialize, comment, or draw conclusions. I just put the facts down in black and white. I gathered my documents and headed over to the office of Clayton's boss, a warrant officer named Len Marco.

I sat down with him, and spelled out the entire situation. "This is what's happening with Harvey," I said. "You can fire me from the course and send me anywhere you want me to go. I would rather stay. But someone needs to shed light on the damage this guy is doing."

I took a deep breath. Had I just committed career suicide?

Len was silent for a few moments, looking at the papers I'd put in front of him as I spelled out the whole story. Then he looked up at me. "Come with me. We need to go talk to Master Chief Jordan."

Master Chief Jordan wasn't just the next higher-up on the navy food chain; he was the master chief in charge of the entire Naval Special Warfare Center. As it happened, he was also the very same Master Chief Jordan who'd been running the sniper course when I had enrolled in it two and a half years earlier. I took this as a good sign. At least he knew me well enough to know that I wasn't making trouble because I had a bad attitude.

On the other hand, he was also the very same master chief who Chief Chris had gone to. I took this as a bad sign.

A very bad sign.

But what could I do? There was no backing out now. Besides, I wouldn't have backed out even if I could. For the course, for the guys, and for myself, this was the right thing to do.

Len started the meeting by explaining in the broadest terms why we were there and then turned it over to me. I went through what I had to say, detailing the worst of Clayton's offenses. Len, to his considerable credit, backed me up. Chief Jordan listened without comment, then nodded slightly and said, "We'll look into this."

We were dismissed.

The next day Clayton started packing. Orders had come down. Apparently there was something of an emergency situation developing in Bahrain where they needed a master chief. Harvey had been assigned to station there unaccompanied for a year.

Instead, he put in for his retirement papers. Within a few weeks Clayton was gone—and suddenly I was not only running the course but also serving in the role of division officer, at least until another interim division officer could be assigned.

In an evaluation Clayton had written up not long before he left, he had said of me, "Promote ahead of his peers!" Ironically, his advice was acted on—after he was gone. In February 2005, just weeks after Clayton left, I made chief petty officer my first time up.

CHAPTER FIFTY-FIVE

With Clayton gone and our new curriculum in place, the sniper course started soaring. We were graduating guys who were absolutely deadly. Suddenly our graduates were in big demand in the field, and I was getting phone calls from other branches of the service. Our guys were gaining such a reputation in combat overseas that officers were saying, "What are these guys doing that we're not doing—and how can we change our course so we start getting our guys to this level?" We were happy to give them all the help we could.

Everything I'd experienced in the navy up to this point had gone into revamping and refining this sniper course. We were now turning out some of the most decorated snipers in the world.

There was no better example of this than Chris Kyle, whose autobiography, *American Sniper*, was turned into an Oscar-nominated movie in 2014.

Chris was a Texan who had been shooting since he was a kid. Like a lot of guys who grew up hunting, he knew how to stalk. He was also a champion rodeo saddle-bronc rider. Actually, the first time he applied to the navy he was flat-out rejected because he had pins in his arm from a serious accident he'd had while in the rodeo ring. The navy later relented and even sought him out for recruitment. That was a good thing for our side, as it turned out.

Chris was one of Eric's students. He immediately made a big impression on all the staff and obviously had great potential, although it didn't jump out at you at first. He was a classic example of a spec ops guy: a book you definitely do not want to judge by its cover. He was a quiet, unassuming, mild-mannered, soft-spoken guy—as long as you didn't get him riled up. If you had walked past Chris Kyle on the street, you would not have had the faintest sense that you'd just strolled by the deadliest marksman in U.S. military history. He had more than 150 confirmed kills.

Like me, when it came time for assignment to the teams, Chris had chosen SEAL Team Three as his top pick—and gotten it. For his first deployment, he was one of the SEALs on the ground in Iraq with the first wave of American troops at the start of Operation Iraqi Freedom in March 2003. While he was there, Chris saw some serious action.

Upon rotating back home, one of the first things Chris did was to go through our sniper course. After graduating, he shipped right back out to Iraq, where he fought in the Second Battle for Fallujah, Iraq. This turned out to be the biggest and bloodiest engagement in the entire Iraq war. Since the largely unsuccessful First Battle for Fallujah seven months earlier, the place had been heavily fortified. We had big army units going in with small sniper teams attached to help give them the edge they needed. Our snipers would sneak in there, see enemy insurgents (sometimes snipers themselves) slipping out to try to ambush our guys, and just drop them in their tracks. It was no contest.

Our guys were not only expert shots, they also knew how to come up with all kinds of creative solutions on the battlefield. For example, they would stage an IED (improvised explosive device) to flush out the enemy. They would take some beat-up vehicle they'd captured in a previous op, rig it with explosives, drive it into the city, and blow it, to make it seem as if it had been hit by an IED. Meanwhile, they would take cover and wait. All these enemy forces would start coming out of the woodwork, shooting off guns and celebrating, "Aha, we got the Americans!" Then our snipers would pick them all off. You didn't hear about this on the news. But it happened, over and over again, throughout the city.

Chris was in the middle of all this. On this deployment, he racked up close to a hundred kills, forty of them in the Second Battle for Fallujah alone. He was shot twice during separate IED explosions, and received multiple frag wounds from explosives.

The insurgents had a sniper there who had been on the Iraqi Olympic shooting team. He was packing an English-made Accuracy International, which was about $10,000 worth of weapon. This guy was not messing around. Neither were Chris and our other snipers. They shot the guy and took his rifle. As a result, al Qaeda put a bounty on Chris's head—but nobody ever collected.

As remarkable as he was, Chris Kyle was quick to point out that he was not unique. There was a whole lineup of SEAL snipers in Iraq at the time who were cutting a wide path through the hotbeds of insurgency. They provided clear zones for our marines and army forces to operate without being picked off by enemy snipers themselves or being ambushed by IEDs.

It's easy to have an image of these guys as trained killers—mean, ruthless men who think nothing of ending other people's lives. Maybe even violent and bloodthirsty. The reality is quite different.

The reality is that the death that comes with the sniper's strike is typically clean, painless, and as humane as death can be. The sniper is like a highly skilled surgeon, only he practices his craft on the battlefield. Make no mistake: war is about killing other human beings. It's about taking out the enemy before he takes you out. It's about stopping the spread of further aggression by stopping those who would perpetuate that aggression. However, if the goal is to do so as fast and effectively as possible, and with the least additional damage, then warriors like Chris Kyle and our other brothers-in-arms are heroes in the very best sense.

CHAPTER FIFTY-SIX

One of our better students was Marcus Luttrell, another Texan and author of his own book, *Lone Survivor*. I mentored both Marcus and his twin brother, Morgan, who came through the course about half a year before Marcus did.

Marcus is the dictionary definition of "conspicuous"—a big, strapping hulk of a guy, colorful, high-spirited, entertaining, and larger than life in every way.

Unfortunately, for a sniper, being noticeable is not necessarily an asset. Like Morgan, Marcus was a first-rate SEAL, but he did not pass through our sniper course without incident. While he was a crack shot, he had a tough time meeting the course minimum requirements for stalking.

I vividly remember the first practice stalk we did with Marcus's class. On these practice stalks we gave the students time to clip off bits and pieces of natural vegetation to put all over their ghillie suits and hats so they would be fully camouflaged. Then they would hide themselves, and we would scan the field to judge how well they were hidden. When we got the sign that everyone was fully vegged up and hidden, I started scanning with my binos. Right away I found myself staring at this odd-looking plant.

As I watched, the plant got to its feet and stood up.

Here was the problem. Plants don't suddenly stand up. Sure enough, it was Marcus, covered with wilting scraps of vegetation. He looked like Bigfoot.

"Oh, man," I remember saying more than once during the course of those practice stalks. "It's Marcus again."

I often took Marcus and his shooting partner out on the course after hours. I quizzed them and worked with them, doing whatever I could to make sure they were getting it.

As much as we all put into it, though, it wasn't enough. Marcus didn't make it. He was crushed, and so were we. He was an excellent shooter and as solid a SEAL as they come, and we all badly wanted to pass him. But we hadn't succeeded in getting him through that concealment and stalking phase.

So what did he do? He turned right around and went through the course a second time. This is a guy who does not know the meaning of the word "quit."

When it came to the stalking portion he started having a rough time again. But this time, at a certain point it just clicked for him. From then on he did really well, and he graduated with flying colors. I don't know who was happier about it, Marcus or us. I'd say we were all pretty fired up.

Right after he graduated, Marcus was deployed to northern Afghanistan. One day he and three teammates—Matt Axelson (Morgan Luttrell's best friend), Danny Dietz, and Michael Murphy—went out on a reconnaissance mission, not far from the area where we had run so many missions with ECHO platoon. The mission went bad, and soon the four were scrambling across the brutal Afghan terrain under heavy fire. Marcus watched as his brother's best friend died in his arms. Murphy and Dietz were killed too. All sixteen of the men (eight SEALs and eight Army Airborne "Night Stalkers") dispatched as a QRF (quick reaction force) to rescue Marcus's team were also killed. It was the worst U.S. loss of life in a single event in Afghanistan—a grisly record of tragedy broken only six years later when a Chinook helo was shot down in August 2011.

We were devastated when we heard the news. I'd lost other friends before, but this was the worst. I'd gotten close to all those guys during the course and had especially come to know Marcus and Axelson really well. Even though Morgan insisted that his twin brother was still alive, most of us believed that Marcus had died too. Five days later we learned that Morgan was right: Marcus had miraculously made it.

Badly wounded, and with all his buddies gone, this big Texan, who had failed stalk after stalk when he first landed in our course, had managed to walk and crawl undetected through some seven miles of hostile terrain, somehow evading capture and killing six more Taliban fighters along the way, until he made it to an Afghan village that shielded him until he could be rescued.

Marcus was the only one out of the entire operation who made it home alive.

The next time I saw Marcus was more than a year later, in the late summer of 2006, on the deck of the USS *Midway* off San Diego where the navy was holding a big fundraiser. I spotted him and went over to talk with him.

We embraced, then quickly caught each other up on what was going on in our lives. There was quite a crowd around us, and we both knew we wouldn't have more than a minute to talk. He grabbed me by both shoulders and said, "Brandon, listen. You need to know, that stalking course? That saved my life. If you hadn't pounded that training into me, I wouldn't be standing here today."

His voice choked, and I saw tears in his eyes. I was getting pretty emotional myself.

"You saved my life, man," he repeated. "I want you to know that, and I want to thank you for it."

I thought about all Marcus had been through in Afghanistan, watching his friends die one by one, the long days and longer nights hidden away in that Afghan village while the Taliban hunted for him, not knowing whether he would make it out alive. I then flashed on all the time I'd spent with Marcus in the course, the hours we put in together long after the day's studies were officially over. I thought about the hours Eric and I and the rest of us had put in crafting and refining that course, the strain on our families while we were away, even the long months of enduring the reign of Harvey Clayton. And I knew that *this* made it all more than worthwhile.

This, without a doubt, was my proudest moment as a Navy SEAL.

EPILOGUE

After running the U.S. Navy SEAL sniper course for two and a half years, I finally decided in mid-2006 to leave the service so I could, in the long run, spend more time with my children. I shortly found myself back in Iraq. This time I was providing mission support as a private contractor. While I was there I rewrote security plans and developed a complete training program for the local security force (who'd had basically no training up to that point). I also ran missions that included delivering attaché cases full of American cash to intel assets (in case you've ever wondered how much $1.5 million in cash weighs, I can tell you: a lot); grabbing double-agent informers in the middle of the night and hauling them in for questioning; arranging and coordinating clandestine meeting points with locals-turned-intel-assets; driving at top speed through the city losing Iranian tails; and anything you might imagine from what you've seen in the movies. I was never ambushed at any of our checkpoints or meeting spots, but it did happen. One group got into a firefight on the road to the city of Kirkuk and had to blast their way through. At another checkpoint, a few of our guys realized too late that the officials on hand were not acting as friendly as they should have been. They got lit up by machine-gun fire and never made it out of there.

By the end of 2007 I was out of Iraq and back in the States, where I began to build my career as an author and digital media entrepreneur. Today my company, Force12 Media, is the largest military content network on the Internet, with websites including NavySEALs.com, SpecialOperations.com, and SOFREP.com, a veteran-run site dedicated to news and opinion on special operations, the military, domestic security, and foreign policy analysis.

Unfortunately, my marriage was not able to survive the intensity and long separations it had endured during my SEAL years. Gabriele and I separated in 2009, and she and our kids took up residence in a nice property within a half-day's drive. We managed it all in as friendly and collaborative a way as anyone could hope for, and we remain committed to having a good relationship, both for the kids' sake and out of respect for ourselves and for each other. I wish it would have worked out better for us, but I've seen friends do far worse. I make a five-hour drive several times a month to spend time with Tyler, Madison, and Jackson, and it's always amazing to see them, every time. The marriage may not have made it, but the family is forever. That is part of my personal red circle.

My dad did well for himself eventually. Not long after I joined the navy he started another company doing spec homes and custom housing, bought some land on the outskirts of Jackson Hole along the Idaho-Wyoming border and developed it, then sank his profits into properties that provided him his retirement. He built a house down in Cabo San Lucas, where he lives in the winter, fishing off the beach and playing drums in a local band. He still plays music every day, and he has a forty-two-foot boat. Our relationship still has that bit of edginess to it. But he's my dad.

My mom and I are still very close, and I see her often. A good number of the memories from the beginning of this book come from her. To this day my parents still talk regularly, and if you asked either of them, I think they would describe themselves as good friends.

I see quite a few of my old SEAL buddies, too, from my Sniper Cell friend Eric to Chief Dan from the GOLF platoon days. I may not be an active member of the teams now, but the community is more like a family than a job, and once you're part of it that never goes away.

The SEAL community was thrust into the public spotlight in April 2009 when a coordinated team of three SEAL snipers took out three Somalian pirates in a perfectly coordinated trio of shots, rescuing Captain Richard Phillips of the *Maersk Alabama*. Soon my phone was ringing off the hook, and before I knew it, I was standing before the CNN cameras explaining to Anderson Cooper the practically impossible logistics involved in pulling off such a mission and the lengths to which those three covert warriors had gone in training for it.

Two years later that spotlight grew more intense when a team of SEALs staged a covert raid on a compound in Pakistan and killed Osama bin Laden, the man credited with orchestrating the 9/11 attacks. Once again I found myself on CNN and other media outlets providing viewers some insights into what had just happened. That sense I'd had back in 2000, standing on the deck of the crippled USS *Cole* off the coast of Yemen, that the nature of the military was tipping upside down and that covert ops forces would soon become the vanguard of twenty-first-century warfare, turned out to be right. Yet I'm not sure the American public fully grasps what that looks like from the inside.

Three months after the bin Laden raid, in August 2011, enemy forces shot down an American helicopter over Afghanistan, killing thirty American special ops troops, including seventeen SEALs. It was the highest number of casualties in a single incident in the war in Afghanistan, higher even than the devastating losses of Operation

Redwing, the op Marcus Luttrell had so narrowly survived. For me, this latest tragedy touched equally close to home. My good friend Heath Robinson, one of the strongest members of our team at ECHO platoon, was one of those seventeen SEALs who died in that helo crash. So was Chris Campbell, a BUD/S classmate of mine. By this time the bin Laden raid had long left the headlines, and most of us in the States were on to other hot news of the day. But the SEALs are not like a sports team who goes off to celebrate and take the season off after winning the Super Bowl. The guys who took out bin Laden were back to work the next day.

Not long ago, I was sitting at the barber's in San Diego getting a haircut when the guy in the next chair looked over at me. It was Chris Ponto, one of the kids I had hung out with in the harbor at Ventura in my teens, back when we were all aimless and hadn't yet figured out what we were going to do with our lives. When I made my decision to get out of there and join the navy, I'd lost touch with them. It was great to catch up. Chris had a boat service going in Ventura. We got to talking about the old days, and I asked him about a guy named Jake who'd been my best friend in those days.

"Jake," said Chris, his eyes dropping to the floor. "He's homeless now. Totally addicted."

Jake was still with the same girlfriend he'd had back then. But he had dragged her down. They were both hanging around the harbor, having a tough time making a living.

Neither Chris nor I said it. But I know we were both thinking the same thing: that could so easily have been me.

I've thought long and hard about why I am writing this book and what I want it to say. I think the message I want my story to get across boils down to two words: excellence matters.

Throughout my time with the navy and within the SEAL community, I've seen poor leadership and exceptional leadership. I've seen training that was simply good, training that was great, and training so amazing it blew my mind. I've seen the difference it makes.

In political matters I have always been a down-the-middle person. When it comes to leaders, I care less about their party affiliation and more about their character and competence. I want to know that they know what they are doing, and that they are made of that kind of unswerving steel that will not be rattled in moments that count, no matter what is coming at them. I want to know that they won't flinch in the face of debate, danger, or death. I want to know that they excel at what they do.

A free society looks like it rests on big principles and lofty ideals, and maybe it does for much of the time. But in the dark times, in those times that count the most, what it comes down to is pure commitment, honed over time into the fabric of excellence.

Why am I telling you this? Because it matters.

You may never shoot a sniper rifle. You may never serve as part of an assault team, or stand security in combat, or board a hostile ship at midnight on the high seas. You may never wear a uniform. You may never even throw a punch in the name of freedom. I'll tell you what, though. Whatever it is that you do, you are making a stand for either mediocrity or excellence.

This is what I learned about being a Navy SEAL. It is all about excellence, and about never giving up on yourself. And that is the red circle I will continue to hold, no matter what.

GLOSSARY

Al Qaeda militant Islamic extremist organization founded by Osama bin Laden

AMU Army Marksmanship Unit, the army's elite shooting team

Atolls coral islands surrounding seawater

Bow front part of a ship or boat

BUD/S Basic Underwater Demolition/SEAL, the Navy SEAL training program

Catamaran a boat with two hulls

Celestial navigation finding one's direction by using the stars

Concealment when you hide behind something that shields you visually, like a bush, but you can still be hit by enemy fire

Cover when you hide behind something that can provide physical protection from enemy fire

Hull main part of a ship or boat

HVT high-value target, a person of interest

Ketch small sailing ship

KIMs keep-in-memory exercises

Mast vertical support for sails

NACCS Naval Air Crew Candidate School

O-course The BUD/S obstacle course

Port left side of a ship or boat

PST physical screening test; all BUD/S candidates must pass this before starting BUD/S

Recon reconnaissance, exploring and gathering information behind enemy lines

SAR Search and Rescue school

SEALS the U.S. Navy's elite special operations force; SEAL stands for sea, air, and land, the ways they are able to literally approach a mission

SERE Survival, Evasion, Resistance, and Escape training, a school all navy pilots and rescue swimmers need to take

SOCOM Special Operations Command, the group that oversees the special operations forces of each branch of the U.S. Armed Forces

SOPMOD kit Special Operations Peculiar Weapons Modificaton kit

Stern rear of a ship or boat

Subsonic slower than the speed of sound

Supersonic faster than the speed of sound

Taliban extremist Islamic movement controlling Afghanistan

Terrorism an act of violence for political reasons

TSO tactical sensor operator

WARCOM Naval Special Warfare Command

WESTPAC deployment to the western Pacific

ACKNOWLEDGMENTS

Writing this memoir has been very personal for me. Exposing your skeletons in the closet and baring your soul to the world can be both humbling and frightening. It reminds me of checking into BUD/S and gazing up at the life-sized "Creature from the Black Lagoon" statue, a gift from some graduating BUD/S class or other, that stands on the quarterdeck greeting all newcomers with its green-mouthed, red-eyed stare. The sign around its neck reads, "So you wanna be a FROGMAN." It's not a question. It's a dare. Like, "So you wanna write a MEMOIR. . . ."

The first time I sat down to discuss this project with my agent, the legendary Margret McBride, in her office in La Jolla, California, she gave me a crucial piece of strategic advice. "Nobody writes his or her own memoir, Brandon," she said. "You're a good writer, but you need a great coauthor to help you out."

I didn't get great; I got incredible. Thank you, John David Mann. Having you as my "swim buddy" on this book project was like having one of my trusted teammates covering me in the field. You took all my scattered notes, napkin files, threads of memories, and countless hours on the phone, and then you turned it all into something truly special. For that I thank you tremendously. We have many sayings in the SEALs. One of them goes, "That guy is solid; I'd take a bullet for him any day," and that's how I feel about John Mann.

The support of so many people goes into any book project, far too many to identify each by name here, but at the top of my list are the following family and friends who will always hold a special place in my heart. Thank you:

To my amazing children; not a day goes by I don't think of the three of you and of how lucky I am to be present in your lives. You inspire me to improve myself and push beyond what I think is possible.

A FEW WORDS FROM MY KIDS

I asked my kids if they wanted to share a few words and here's what they said:

"Doing it for yourself is great, but doing it for others is amazing." —*Jackson*

"When life gives you lemonade, make pineapple juice, and keep the world wondering how you did it."—*Madison, aka Livie*

"Never give up; you'll get there."—*Tyler, aka G-man*

To my mother, Lynn, for not giving me up for adoption in those early years in Canada (!) and for always being there for me, rain or shine.

To my dad, Jack, for being there for those early-morning sporting events; it meant a lot to me.

To my sister, Maryke, who runs my Red Circle Foundation. You're the best!

To my ex-wife, for being a great friend and amazing co-parent, and mom to our wonderful kids.

To my family in Canada.

To Eric Davis, for your friendship and hard and innovative work at the SEAL sniper course.

To the men of SEAL Team Three GOLF and ECHO platoons; you know who you are.

To Travis Lively, for proving that brotherhood still exists.

To Thomas Frasher, for always being there when it counted. You're a true brother.

To Johnny "Tsunami" Surmont, one of the most creative SEALs I know, always inventing something new. You've been a great friend, Johnny—keep making great things!

To Billy Tosheff, my friend and fellow aviator. Thanks for everything, brother. Not too many friends will show up at 2:00 A.M., no questions asked!

To Alex Tosheff, for believing in my site and the business potential of SOFREP.com. You are Tier One IT, my friend!

To Jack Murphy, Charlie Jackman, Ian Scotto, and all the guys at SOFREP; you define the word "excellence."

To Master Chief Manty, for teaching me what it means to be a chief.

To Master Chief Jason Gardner, for your support and knowledge in all things sniper.

To fellow teammate Rob Smith and his lovely wife, Nicole. It never ceases to amaze me how creative guys in our SOF community are. Rob, your handmade RESCO instruments are incredible, and I've gladly put my Rolex out to pasture in favor of my new RESCO. Thanks for keeping the brotherhood alive and working with me on the signature "Red Circle" RESCO watch.

To Bill Magee, owner of the dive boat *Peace*. Some of my fondest childhood memories are of time on that boat with you and the crew.

To Marc Resnick, our editor at St. Martin's, for believing in this book before it even existed, and to our literary agent, Margret McBride, for helping to make it happen.

To Thea Feldman, for her excellent and sensitive hand in adapting this book for younger readers.

To Marcus Luttrell and his wife, Melanie (I know who's in charge).

To the WindanSea Surf Club, for welcoming me into their clan.

Finally I want to acknowledge the following fallen SEAL teammates who touched my life in both training and combat. You guys will live in my memories forever: Matt "Axe" Axelson, Mike Bearden, Chris Campbell, Glen Doherty, Jason Freiwald, Chris Kyle, Mike Murphy, Tom Retzer, Heath Robinson, Dave Scott, Jon "JT" Tumilson, John Zinn, and honorary teammates Mike Dahan and Paulo Emanuele.

See you on the other side, gents.

BRANDON

INDEX

Abraham Lincoln, USS, 46–47, 49, 53

Afghanistan, xv, 177
American helicopter shot down in, 211–12
Luttrell in, x, 205–7
Operation Enduring Freedom in, xv, 152
Webb in operations in, 152–74
Zhawar Kili complex in, 158–74

Afghan United Front, 152
Agio, 11–12, 13, 18–23
aim, natural point of, 107
Ali (senior corpsman), 144
Alpha-117, 148–51
al Qaeda, xiv–xv, 215
Cole attacked by, xiii–xv, 138, 139–41, 147, 211
embassies attacked by, 148, 149
Kyle and, 202
Operation Enduring Freedom against, xv, 152
September 11, 2001 attacks by, xv, 138, 145–46, 155, 162, 211
Zhawar Kili complex and, 158–74

American Sniper (Kyle), 200
anchors, 21–22
Animals, 17, 26
antisubmarine warfare operator (AW), 42
area of operations (AO), 88
Army Marksmanship Unit (AMU), 106–7, 215
"A" school, 42
atolls, 215
Axelson, Matt "Axe," x, 205–6

Bagram Air Base, 161, 174
Bahrain, 138, 139, 198
ballistics, 103, 115–16, 121, 187
Basic Underwater Demolition/SEAL training (BUD/S), ix, xviii, xix, 34, 35, 42, 45, 47, 52–54, 60–87, 88, 89, 102, 144, 178, 179, 215

Basic Underwater Demolition/SEAL
     training (BUD/S) (*continued*)
  brass bell in, 59, 62, 71, 73, 74
  chow runs in, 74
  classroom in, 77
  Demo Pit in, 75
  dive phase of, 76–77
  First Phase of, 60, 61–63, 64–67,
     68–69, 70–72, 73–75, 76
  Goon Squad in, 65
  graduation from, 86
  "gray man" saying in, 72
  guns in, 85
  Hell Week in, 69, 70, 71–72, 73–75,
     77, 80
  indoctrination phase of, 60, 61
  land navigation training in, 80–81
  meals in, 82–83
  mental strength tested in, 71, 74
  O-course in, 65–67, 79, 216
  phases of, 60
  physical screening test (PST) in,
     57–59, 61, 216
  Pool Comp test in, 77–78
  PT training in, 62, 63, 69, 81
  Round the World exercise in, 74–75
  Second Phase of, 60, 76–78
  steel pier exercise in, 73
  surf hit in, 77
  surf zone in, 62–63, 74
  "that guy" saying in, 63, 72, 89
  Third Phase of, 60, 79–81, 82–85
  thoughts of quitting, 71
  timed runs in, 81
  water skills training in, 68–69
  Webb's graduation from, 86–87
  Webb's leg injury and, 81, 83
  whammy in, 77–78
  Zodiac exercise in, 83–85
Bassham, Lanny, 191–92
Bearden, Mike, 126

bin Laden, Osama, xiv–xv, 148, 158,
     162, 215
  killing of, 134, 211, 212
Black Hawk, 46
Blair, Tony, 152
bomb damage assessment (BDA), 159
boot camp, 43
  Webb in, 31–33, 34–35, 36, 39, 43,
     54
bow, 215
Brad (Combat Controller), 159, 163,
     165, 167
Brad (EOD tech), 156–57, 159
breathing, 107, 110
Buchanan, Instructor, 62, 71
Burkitt, Lieutenant, 49–51
Bush, George W., 152
Bysh, Chris, 10

camouflage:
  ghillie suits and hats, 127–28, 129,
     204–5
  hide sites, 129
  of rifles, 128
Camp Atterbury, 186
Campbell, Chris, 212
Camp Doha, 145, 147
Camp Pendleton, 95, 105–6
Carver, Seth, 104
Cassidy, Chris, 149, 150, 154, 165,
     166, 167, 170, 171, 172
catamaran, 215
celestial navigation, 20, 215
check ride, 47–48
Chemical Reconnaissance Detach-
     ment (CRD), 159
Chris, Chief, 195, 196, 198
Chris (SEAL colleague), 144, 147, 149,
     172, 173
chronographs, 187–88
Clarin, Bruce, 52–53

Clayton, Harvey, 193–96, 197–99, 200, 207
CNN, 211
Coalinga Rifle Club, 103, 106
Coalition, 153, 155
cold bore shots, 109–11, 112–13
Cole, USS, xiii–xv, 138, 139–41, 147, 211
Combat Controllers (CCTs), 159
commanding officer (CO), 51
concealment, 215
  cover vs., 90–91
Cooper, Anderson, 211
Coriolis effect, 123–24
Coronado, 100
Counterterrorist Intelligence Center (CTIC), 159
cover, 216
  concealment vs., 90–91
crosshairs (reticles), 121–22

Dan, Chief, 100, 211
Davis, Eric, 179, 183, 185, 186, 188, 193, 201, 207, 211
dead space, 128, 132
demolition training, 92, 93
Demo Pit, 75
Department of Defense, xiv
desert warfare training, 92–93
Dietz, Danny, 205–6
distance:
  long-distance targets, 123–24
  range estimation, 165–66
  unknown, 121–22, 125–26
DNA, 159, 163, 165
Dodd, Scott, 10
dreams, pursuing, xviii, xix, 32–33
drown-proofing, 41, 68
Duluth, USS, 137–41, 142
Dye, Chris, 143, 164, 165, 172, 173

Earth, rotation of, 123–24
ECHO platoon, 142–44, 145–47, 148–51, 205, 212
edge shots, 111
Eric (Combat Controller), 159, 163
excellence, 212–13
Explosive Ordnance Disposal (EOD), 154, 156–57

Fallujah:
  First Battle for, 201
  Second Battle for, 201–2
FBI, 159, 163
final firing position (FFP), 128, 130, 131, 132, 133
first-line gear, 79
flight simulators, 39
Force12 Media, 210
forward-looking infrared (FLIR), 147, 149
Fries, Rich, 49–51
Frog Hill, 83

Gardner, Chief, 178, 179, 183, 184, 185, 186
ghillie suits and hats, 127–28, 129, 204–5
Glen (colleague), 100, 103, 105, 134
  Cole attack and, 139, 141, 147
  as Webb's sniper partner, 119–20, 125–26
glossary, 215–17
golf, 131
GOLF platoon, 99–100, 105, 134, 142, 143, 211
Goon Squad, 65
Guantánamo prison camp, 153
guns, see weapons and shooting

hapkido, 67
Harward, Captain, 163–65

Helicopter Anti-Submarine Squadron
    Six (HS-6), 46–48, 49–51
Helicopter Anti-Submarine Squadron
    Ten (HS-10), 43, 46
Hell Week, 69, 70, 71–72, 73–75, 77, 80
Helo Support at TRADET, 179–81,
    183
H-gear, 79
hide sites, 129
high-value targets (HVTs), 148, 216
Hilo, Hawaii, 24–26
Himalayas, x
Hindu Kush, x
Hiva Oa, 20–21
Hrabak, James, 162
hull, 216
hunting, 183–84

improvised explosive device (IED),
    202
Instructor Training School, 181–82
Iran, 137
Iraq, xv, 137, 145, 201, 202
    Alpha-117 and, 148–51
    Desert Storm and, 146
    First Battle for Fallujah, 201
    Operation Iraqi Freedom and, 201
    Second Battle for Fallujah, 201–2
    Webb as private contractor in,
        209–10
iron sights, 106, 109

Jake (friend), 212
JDAM (puppy), 169
Joint Direct Attack Munition
    (JDAMs), 159, 167
Jordan, Master Chief, 198

Kabul, 152
Kandahar International Airport, 153,
    155, 174

keep-in-memory exercises (KIMs),
    114–15, 188, 216
Kennedy (copilot), 49–51
Kentucky windage, 166
ketch, 216
Khost, 158
killed in action (KIA), 172
Kitty Hawk, USS, 53, 61
knot-tying trial, 69
Kowalski, Instructor, 67
Kuwait, 145, 147, 154
Kyle, Chris, 200–203

Laguna Mountains, 80
land navigation training, 80–81
Land Warfare at TRADET, 178
La Posta Mountains, 89
laser rangefinders, 122, 129
laser sights, PEQ, 124
Lone Survivor (Luttrell), xi, 204
long-distance targets, 123–24
Luttrell, Marcus, ix–xi, 204–7, 212
Luttrell, Morgan, 204, 205

Maersk Alabama, 211
Magee, Bill, 15, 17, 18, 20, 24, 26, 41
marching drills, 32
Marco, Len, 197–98
maritime operations (MAROPS), 178
Marquesas Islands, 20, 22
mast, 216
McNary, Lieutenant, 100, 103
McRaven, William, 134
memorization, 188
    keep-in-memory exercises (KIMs),
        114–15, 188, 216
mental strength and management,
    71, 74, 191–92
Midway, USS, 206
mirage, 108
moving targets, 121

Multiple Integrated Laser Engagement System (MILES), 93
Murphy, Michael, 205–6

Nairobi, 148, 149
National Security Agency (NSA), 148, 149
NATO, 137
Naval Air Crew Candidate School (NACCS), 35, 37, 39–40, 216
Naval Special Warfare Center, 198
Naval Special Warfare Command (WARCOM), 185, 193, 217
Naval Special Warfare Group One, 134
Naval Special Warfare Group One Training Detachment (TRADET), 177–79, 185, 186
　Helo Support, 179–81, 183
　Land Warfare, 178
　Sniper Cell, 178–79, 184, 185
　Webb at, 177–79, 184, 185, 186
Naval Special Warfare sniper school, ix–x, 100–134, 198
　aiming training in, 107
　Army Marksmanship Unit and, 106–7
　ballistics study in, 103, 115–16, 121, 187
　breathing training in, 107, 110
　butts area in, 114, 120
　classroom work in, 114, 115
　Coalinga Rifle Club and, 103, 106
　dropout rate in, 103, 125, 190
　final test in, 103, 134
　graduation ceremony in, 134
　keep-in-memory exercises in, 114–15
　qualifying shoot for, 105–6
　redesigning of course in, 104, 185–89, 190–92, 200

　running to target exercise in, 110–11
　shooter and spotter pairs in, 103, 119–20, 125–26
　shooting phase in, 103–26
　snaps and movers tests in, 120–21, 125–26
　stalking drills in, 129
　stalking phase in, 103, 126, 127–34
　stress orchestrated in, 120
　target sketching in, 115
　unknown distance tests in, 121–22, 125–26
　Webb as manager of, 193–96, 197, 200–203, 209
　Webb's first shooting test in, 119
　Webb's graduation from, 134
　see also weapons and shooting
Naval Training Center (NTC), 31–33, 34–35, 36, 39, 89, 183
Navy SEALs, x, xiv, xviii, 16, 17, 216
　bin Laden killed by, 134, 211, 212
　ECHO platoon, 142–44, 145–47, 148–51, 205, 212
　GOLF platoon, 99–100, 105, 134, 142, 143, 211
　in helicopter shot down in Afghanistan, 211–12
　90/10 rule in, 143
　probation period for, 88
　reorganization of, 178
　reputation and, 89–90
　Somalian pirates and, 211
　Team Three, 88, 137–41, 178, 201
　Tridents of, 88, 95–96, 99
　Webb in, see Webb, Brandon, as Navy SEAL
　Webb's training for, see Webb, Brandon, SEAL training of
Nicklaus, Jack, 131
Nielson, Chief, 186, 193, 194

Niland, 92–94, 95, 103, 127, 128, 131–32, 134

9/11 attacks, xv, 138, 145–46, 155, 162, 211

NYFD, 146

Ocean Hawk, 46

O-course, 65–67, 79, 216

Olson, Eric T., 134

operational readiness exam (ORE), 100

Operation Desert Storm, 146

Operation Enduring Freedom, xv, 152

Operation Iraqi Freedom, 201

Operation Neptune's Spear, 134

Operation Redwing, 211–12

Oppositional Force (OppFor) exercises, 93

Pakistan, 158, 169, 171

Papeete, Tahiti, 22, 25

Peace, 15–17, 18, 25, 26, 37, 41

Persian Gulf, 137, 145

Phillips, Richard, 211

photographic intelligence course (PIC), 187

physical screening test (PST), 57–59, 61, 216

physical training (PT), 32, 35, 39, 40, 62, 63, 69, 81

Ponto, Chris, 212

Pool Comp, 77–78

port, 216

prisoner of war (POW) camp simulation, 43–45, 153

quick reaction force (QRF), 206

range estimation, 165–66

Rasmussen, Gaytor, 10

reconnaissance, 216

reputation, 89–90

reticles, 121–22

rigid-hulled inflatable boats (RHIBs), 150

Roach, Michael, 15, 16, 17, 20

Robinson, Heath, 212

Rock, 82

Round the World, 74–75

rules of engagement (ROE), 153

Rural Training, 183–84

Saddam Hussein, xv, 137, 146

San Clemente Island, 82, 100, 179, 180

Sea Hawks, 46, 147, 149

SEALs, *see* Navy SEALs

SEAL Tactical Training (STT), 89–96, 102

    desert warfare training in, 92–93

    stress courses in, 89–91

    Webb's graduation from, 95–96

Search and Rescue (SAR), 35, 40–41, 42, 68, 89, 216

second-line gear, 79

September 11, 2001 attacks, xv, 138, 145–46, 155, 162, 211

SERE, *see* Survival, Evasion, Resistance, and Escape

Shilo, 24–26

Shoulin, Instructor, 69, 70–71, 85, 86–87

snaps and movers test, 120–21, 125–26

Sniper Cell at TRADET, 178–79, 184, 185

snipers, 26, 202

    most important traits and skills in, 172–73, 191

Somalia, 183

Somalian pirates, 211

Special Operations Command (SOCOM), x, 134, 217

special operations forces, xiv, xv
    growing importance of, xv, 178, 211
Special Operations Peculiar Weapons
    Modification (SOPMOD), 185–86,
    217
stern, 217
Steve (EOD tech), 156, 159, 163, 164
stress courses, 89–91
STT, *see* SEAL Tactical Training
subsonic, 217
supersonic, 217
Survival, Evasion, Resistance, and
    Escape (SERE), 43–45, 153, 216
swordfish, 25–26

tactical operations center (TOC), 163
tactical sensor operator (TSO), 47–48,
    49, 217
Tahiti, 22, 24, 25
Taliban, xv, 217
    Luttrell and, x, 206, 207
    Operation Enduring Freedom
        against, xv, 152
    Zhawar Kili complex and, 158–74
Tanzania, 148, 149
target sketching, 115
Tarnak Farms, 155
Task Force K-Bar, 153
technology, 190, 194
    in training, 187
    in weapons, 187–88
terrorism, xiv–xv, 140, 217
third-line gear, 79
Tomaszeski, Steven John, 53
Tora Bora, 158, 174
torture, 74
TRADET, *see* Naval Special Warfare
    Group One Training Detachment

Underwater Demolition Team
    (UDT), 59

Underwater Demolition Training, *see*
    Basic Underwater Demolition/
    SEAL training
underwater skills training, 68–69
    dive phase, 76–77
United Nations, 137
unknown distance test, 121–22,
    125–26
Urban Sniper Training, 183

veg fan, 128
Ventura, Calif., 11, 212

WARCOM (Naval Special Warfare
    Command), 185, 193, 217
warfare, xiii–xv, 202–3
    growing importance of special
        operations in, xv, 178, 211
water, 163, 164, 168
weapons and shooting, 89
    ballistics and, 103, 115–16, 121, 187
    bullet's top arc and, 117
    chronographs and, 187–88
    cold bore shots and, 109–11, 112–13
    edge shots and, 111
    final firing position in, 128, 130,
        131, 132, 133
    flight path and, 116–17
    iron sights on, 106, 109
    laser rangefinders and, 122, 129
    long-distance targets and, 123–24
    losing of, 85, 143
    machine guns, 92–93
    malfunctions and, 118–19
    measurements and calculations in,
        122
    moving targets and, 121
    natural point of aim and, 107
    PEQ laser sights and, 124
    reticles and, 121–22
    scoped weapons, 118–19, 121

weapons and shooting (*continued*)
  sights and, 106, 109, 124
  SOPMOD kit upgrade, 185–86
  in stress courses, 89–91
  submachine guns, 89
  technology and, 187–88
  see also Naval Special Warfare
    sniper school
weapons of mass destruction (WMD),
  xv
Webb, Brandon:
  as author and entrepreneur, 210
  baseball playing of, 6, 10, 15
  birth of, 4
  boat job on the *Peace,* 15–17, 18,
    25, 26, 37, 41
  childhood of, xvii–xviii, xix, 4–7,
    8–12, 13–14
  childhood savings account of, 9
  children of, 6, 99, 177, 210
  diving of, 16–17, 22, 26, 27, 37, 76
  family moves during childhood,
    xvii, 9–10, 11
  in high school, 14–15, 18, 20
  hockey playing of, 14
  instructor training of, 181–82
  knee problems of, 14
  Lake Tahoe trip with family, xix
  leg injury of, 81, 83
  as private contractor in Iraq, 209–10
  as rescue diver, 17, 37
  skiing of, 5–6
  thrown off boat by father, 3, 23,
    24, 25, 134
  on world-encircling sailing trip,
    18–23
  wrestling of, 6, 10, 15
Webb, Brandon, as Navy SEAL:
  in Afghanistan, 152–74
  as chief petty officer (E-7), 194, 199
  earns Trident, 96

  in ECHO platoon, 142–44, 145–47,
    148–51, 205, 212
  first deployment as sniper, 137–41,
    142
  as goal, xviii, 27, 32–33, 36, 37, 58
  in GOLF platoon, 99–100, 105, 134,
    142, 143, 211
  as petty officer first class (E-6),
    184, 194
  proudest moment of, 207
  reenlistment bonus and, 142
  in redesigning of sniper school
    course, 104, 185–89, 190–92, 200
  service left by, 209
  as sniper course manager, 193–96,
    197, 200–203, 209
  in SOPMOD kit upgrade, 185–86
  at TRADET, 177–79, 184, 185, 186
Webb, Brandon, SEAL training of,
  88, 89–100
  at BUD/S, *see* Basic Underwater
    Demolition/SEAL training
  at Naval Air Crew Candidate
    School, 35, 37, 39–40
  at Naval Special Warfare sniper
    school, *see* Naval Special
    Warfare sniper school
  at Naval Training Center, 31–33,
    34–35, 36, 39, 89
  at SEAL Tactical Training, *see*
    SEAL Tactical Training
  at Search and Rescue, 35, 40–41,
    42, 68, 89
  at Survival, Evasion, Resistance,
    and Escape, 43–45, 153
Webb, Gabriele (wife), 99, 145, 177, 210
Webb, Jack (father), 3–7, 8–12, 13–14,
    36–38, 210
  bankruptcy of, 8–10, 11
  Brandon thrown off boat by, 3, 23,
    24, 25, 134